## A Historical and Biblical Refutation of Black Hebrew Israelite Doctrine

*Another Gospel*

Copyright © 2026 by DR. JAMES L. PERRY, SR.

All rights reserved. No part of this book may be reproduced or transmitted in any form or by any means without the author's prior written permission.

Scripture quotations are from the Holy Bible, unless otherwise noted.

ISBN: 979-8-23404-149-4

# Dedication

First and foremost, this book is dedicated to my Lord and Savior, Jesus Christ, who has rescued me from the penalty of sin and prepared me to defend the gospel. This book is also dedicated to those who are set for the defense of the gospel and who have been misled by counterfeit gospels, and to every person seeking truth with humility and courage. I am also thankful for my lovely wife, Cynthia Perry, and my three beautiful children, Priscilla, James Jr., and Jonathan, who make my life complete as an inheritance from the Lord. Lastly, I dedicate this book to my mentor, confidant, and spiritual father, John A. James, also known as Johnny James "The Walking Bible," who has been the most significant influence in my journey with Christ and has taught me the importance of scriptural integrity and dedication to the study of God's word. He inspired me to write this book and many more to come. You will never know how much I miss you and how much I cherish the memories we shared as the LORD used you to mold me into the man I am today.

# Table of Contents

## Foreword

The modern movement often called "Black Hebrew Israelites" (BHI) is diverse, ranging from communities that are largely cultural or restorative to groups that preach an explicitly racialized, exclusivist gospel.[1] This book focuses on the latter: the street-corner and internet-driven ideologies that claim prophetic authority, redefine salvation along ethnic lines, and weaponize Scripture against both Jews and Christians.

Many of its themes are understandable responses to real trauma, slavery, Jim Crow, lynching, and the long history of dehumanization. However, sincere pain does not turn error into truth. When any movement claims that God's covenant promises are possessed by one modern ethnicity alone and that Christ's gospel is insufficient without racial pedigree, it has crossed from cultural memory into "another gospel" (Gal. 1:6–9).

My hope is not to mock, but to clarify. If the Scriptures are handled carefully, they provide resources both to honor African history and to reject the racial mythology that masquerades as biblical faith. The God of Abraham is not a tribal deity whom modern racial categories can capture. In Christ, God forms a new humanity (Eph. 2:11–22), and he judges every ideology, white supremacy, Black supremacy, and every other supremacy by the cross.

---

[1] Miller, Michael T. Black Hebrew Israelites. Cambridge University Press, 2024.

## Preface

This manuscript is written for three audiences: (1) readers who have encountered BHI claims and want a calm, sourced response; (2) believers who love Scripture but feel shaken by confident proof-texting; and (3) anyone who has been told that faith in Christ is not enough unless one belongs to a particular bloodline. Throughout, I distinguish between the historical realities of African peoples and the theological claims of modern BHI sects. The first should be celebrated; the second should be tested and, where found false, rejected.

The approach is straightforward: we examine key BHI arguments, ask what the Bible actually says in context, compare the claims with what historians and scholars can responsibly affirm, and then offer a Christian response rooted in the gospel.

## Introduction

From the earliest days of the transatlantic slave trade, the Bible shaped how enslaved Africans and their descendants made sense of suffering and hope. The Exodus story, in particular, became a powerful framework for endurance, protest, and visions of freedom.

This book is titled "Fallacies of the Self-Proclaimed Black Hebrew Israelites," and 1 Timothy 4:1 is referenced because the doctrine of the self-proclaimed BHI emerged only in the 19th century. This is a doctrine that has developed in these latter days, and the apostle Paul informed Timothy: "Now the Spirit speaketh expressly, that in the latter times some shall depart from the faith, giving heed to seducing spirits, and doctrines of devils" (1 Tim. 4:1, KJV).[2] Harry Rimmer, in his book titled "The Magnificence of Jesus," stated, "If it is new, it is not true."[3] I believe this because the doctrinal foundation laid in the Holy Scriptures does not support these teachings, and there is no new revelation to the Church of the Living God. This book will demonstrate how these teachings are flawed through an exegesis of scripture and historical apologetics.

The self-proclaimed BHI has entered into fallacies based on objective information derived from a historical text in the Bible that has become a figment of their imagination. This claim lacks factual support and is merely a preconceived notion, unsupported by scholarly evidence. There are too many holes in their message to consider it absolute truth. Still, they consist of a dogma that is racially motivated and has brainwashed many who have reacted only because of their marginalization and disenfranchisement. This is no more than an adverse reaction to the harsh conditions of racism in the United States of America against African Americans, which has thwarted

---

[2] Miller, Michael T., 2019. "Black Judaism(s) and the Hebrew Israelites", Religion Compass(11), 13. https://doi.org/10.1111/rec3.12346

[3] Harry Rimmer if its new it's not true.

the image of black people as no more than subservient to the white race. This movement is not unique in its kind but has similar undertones to the Nation of Islam, which both share a black supremacist identity. Although African Americans do need a stimulus in their self-esteem, self-efficacy, and self-worth, this is not the correct process by creating an image that does not belong to their race. It does more damage than it does good because the identity of the African American continues to be on an ever-swinging pendulum of identity crisis, and this has caused another great heave-ho that will not allow the identity of the African American to come to grips with who they are and where they come from. Is it such an awful existence of the African American people that they do not want to take pride in who they are, but instead will gravitate towards multiple identities of other races to escape the horrors of our ancestors who were in slavery, and fail to look past slavery to a rich culture of people that established great kingdoms in the motherland of Africa that had well established nations and great kingdoms long before Israel was became a nation! We must beware of this deceptive doctrine lest their strong conviction deceive us and we fall into their traps of illusions. They have painted everything black, not realizing that life is not so black-and-white. The same accusation that black people accuse white people of white-washing everything, the Self-proclaimed Hebrew Israelites have black-washed everything. The use of the word black can be very deceiving to the degree that we use black to describe people of color who descend from the African slaves who were brought from the continent of Africa. However, to use this term loosely as if everybody who came from Africa was black is fraudulent and unlearned because Africa has 53 different countries. Not everybody comes from the same haplogroup and shares a common ancestor. Two-thirds of the world's population is considered to be people of color, but this does not mean that everyone is black. When Jesus fled to Egypt, he fled to an Egypt that had already been conquered by Alexander the Great more than 300 years earlier. This was a place that had already been colonized with Greek culture and people, so to use Jesus fleeing to Egypt as proof that he blended in as a black man is extremely hypothetical. If he were a person of color, this does not mean that he was a black man whose identity matches that of black people in America. We will discuss this in more depth in the chapter on genealogy and haplogroups. This book will highlight facts that the self-proclaimed BHI failed to acknowledge and open readers' minds to other facts that will challenge its fallacies.

The tragedy is that the same Scriptures that sustained faith can also be twisted into tools of domination, whether by slaveholders who cited isolated verses to defend oppression, or by modern movements that invert the logic of supremacy and baptize ethnocentrism as "Hebrew truth." This book argues that racialized identity claims are not the heart of biblical Israel, and they are not the heart of the Christian gospel.

# Chapter 1: Historical Origins and the Modern BHI Movement

## From Post-Emancipation Trauma to New Religious Movements

Most Black Hebrew Israelite (BHI) streams are best explained not by an ancient, traceable migration of Israelites into West Africa and then into the Americas but by late-nineteenth and early-twentieth-century Black religious creativity in the United States, forged in the pressure-cooker of Reconstruction's collapse, lynching culture, and the hardening architecture of Jim Crow.[4] In that setting, new religious movements often formed around a shared need: to restore dignity, narrate suffering, and reclaim identity in a society that was determined to deny all three. The United States was forged in the pressure-cooker of Reconstruction's collapse, the rise of Jim Crow, and the search for dignity in an age of racial terror.[5]

Scholarly descriptions of "Black Judaism" (a broader category that includes Hebrew Israelite expressions) repeatedly emphasize that these communities were shaped by the social and religious environment of Black America's sentiment: independent church-building, Holiness currents, Black nationalism, and the existential need for an identity that white supremacy could not cancel.[6] One analysis explicitly notes how frustration with Jim Crow laws and the strengthening of independent Black churches created fertile ground for the emergence of this kind of religious expression, while also rejecting the notion that it arose because Jewish slaveholders

---

[4] Kosba, M. T. *The Race Question: Egyptian Intellectualism on the Periphery of the African Diaspora.* 2022.

[5] Jimmy Butts, "Origin and Insufficiency of the Black Hebrew Israelite Movement," Christian Research Institute (CRI), PDF.

[6] Butts, "Origin and Insufficiency of the Black Hebrew Israelite Movement," on Jim Crow era influences and Black church development.

evangelized enslaved Africans (in part because synagogues typically denied Black membership).[7]

In other words, the movement's energy is historically intelligible. People in pain, especially those with systemic, generational pain, search for explanatory frameworks. The Hebrew Bible offers a powerful set of themes: bondage, covenant, identity, divine judgment, deliverance, and promised restoration. For many African Americans, biblical Israel's story did not merely resemble their experience; it felt like the only story in the dominant culture that took their suffering seriously and promised that oppression would not have the last word.

**Post-Emancipation Trauma and the "Identity Problem"**

After Emancipation, Black life in America did not "open up" into a free and equal society. Instead, Black communities often faced a brutal reconfiguration of control: convict leasing, disenfranchisement, lynching, segregation, and economic exclusion. The resulting trauma was not only physical and political; it was also existential. Enslavement had violently fractured language, lineage, homeland, and the ordinary means of knowing "who we are" and "where we come from." That fracture helps explain why identity-based religious movements flourished.

One scholarly framing, cited in the material you have already collected, argues that "Black Judaism" functioned primarily as Black social protest more than as an organic continuation of normative Jewish expression; it also distinguishes between Black people who converted to normative Judaism and those who developed "Black Judaism" as a distinct religious movement with its own emphases and aims. That distinction matters because it clarifies what the earliest founders were doing: they were not

---

[7] Isaac, W. "Locating Afro-American Judaism: A Critique of White Normativity." A Companion to African-American Studies, Wiley Online Library, 2006.

producing genealogical histories so much as constructing a sacred identity capable of resisting cultural degradation.

This is where BHI's origins become pastorally and historically important. In many cases, the shift was from symbolic identification ("we are like Israel") to literalized identity ("we are Israel"), turning a powerful analogy into a genealogical certainty that could not easily be tested.[8]

## Early Founders: Revelation as the "Identity Engine"

The modern movement's early architects are consistently identified in scholarship as Frank S. Cherry and William Saunders Crowdy figures whose claims were grounded not in documentary evidence of lineage but in revelatory certainty and community formation.[9]

Cherry claimed to have received a vision instructing him to proclaim that African Americans were the true descendants of the biblical Hebrews; this catalyzed the establishment of the Church of the Living God, the Pillar Ground of Truth for All Nations.[10]

The same source describes Crowdy's emergence in the era of lynching and Jim Crow: he claimed a revelation that African Americans were descendants of ancient Israelites and founded the Church of God and Saints of Christ (1896, Kansas), explicitly connecting Black identity to the narrative of the "Ten Lost Tribes."[11]

These two stories of origin are crucial to the argument because they show the mechanism at the center of early BHI identity formation:

Authority is anchored in revelation, not in verifiable history.

---

[8] Michael T. Miller, "Black Judaism(s) and the Hebrew Israelites," Religion Compass 13, no. 11 (2019): e12346.

[9] Anderson, C. L. The Storied Landscape of Iroquoia: History and Memory on the New York Frontier, 1750–1840. 2012.

[10] Butts, "Origin and Insufficiency of the Black Hebrew Israelite Movement," on Frank S. Cherry's vision claim and founding of the Church of the Living God (c. 1886).

[11] Butts, "Origin and Insufficiency of the Black Hebrew Israelite Movement," on William Saunders Crowdy's revelation claim and founding of the Church of God and Saints of Christ (1896).

Community is anchored in a re-narration of identity, not in demonstrated genealogy.

The claim "we are Israel" functions as a sacred reversal of social degradation.

This does not make early leaders "frauds" in a simplistic sense. It does mean that the movement's foundational proposition is, historically speaking, a modern religious claim, born in modern conditions, and therefore must be evaluated as such, especially when later versions insist that dissent is "denying the truth."

**Urbanization, the Great Migration, and Harlem's Religious Laboratories**

As the movement spread, it did so in tandem with major demographic shifts. The transatlantic slave trade and the Great Migration transported millions of Black Southerners to Northern cities.[12] Urban life, industrial schedules, crowded housing, political machines, new forms of poverty, and new forms of opportunity created both disorientation and possibility. The city could feel like exile, but it could also function like Jerusalem-in-waiting: a place where new institutions could be built.

During the twentieth century, self-organized African American congregations such as the Moorish Zionist Temple and the Commandment Keepers (both of Harlem) styled themselves as authentic Jewish congregations with rabbis and Torah scrolls, drawing attention from the broader Jewish community. Importantly, early scholarly investigations in the 1960s often concluded that these "Black Jews" were not historically descended from Jews, but were groups ultimately descended from African American Christians who found a mirror of their slavery and segregation experience in the biblical narratives of bondage and liberation, and who

---

[12] Eltis, David. "A brief overview of the Trans-Atlantic Slave Trade." Voyages: The trans-atlantic slave trade database 2007 (2007): 1700-1810.

sought an identity to replace what had been stolen through the Middle Passage.

Hidden ancient migrations do not best explain the movement; rather, it is a matter of modern identity reconstruction under pressure.

**A Movement, or Many Movements?**

One of the chronic difficulties in writing about BHI is the tendency (especially in popular coverage) to treat "Black Hebrew Israelites" as a single organization with a single theology. Historically, it is more accurate to speak of overlapping families of groups that share motifs of identity, covenant, commandments, and a prophetic reading of Black suffering, but that diverge sharply in doctrine and social posture.

The same scholarly overview underscores this point: "movement may be the wrong word; there is very little unity," even though certain motifs persist across decades. It is important to understand that the goal is not to "paint with one brush," but to track how a recognizable set of ideas emerges, spreads, and mutates. Any serious critique must keep that diversity in view while still naming the recurring error: using "Israel" as a basis for superiority rather than covenant faithfulness.[13]

It is important to distinguish:

- Israelite-identity congregations that seek Jewish authenticity and sometimes move toward normative Judaism.

- Messianic-oriented Israelite groups that confess Jesus in some form while also emphasizing law/identity.

- Exclusivist/racialized sects that weaponize identity, deny Jewish legitimacy, and/or redefine the gospel as lineage.

---

[13] Mohamed, Hani Abdirachid, 2023. "African Civilization: From Ancient Kingdoms to Modern Societies", International Journal of Social Science and Human Research(06), 06. https://doi.org/10.47191/ijsshr/v6-i6-11

There is a "frequent transition" between general Hebrew Israelite membership and normative Black Jewish communities; some individuals "discover" Hebrew identity through street-preaching groups and later convert to rabbinic Judaism. They also describe international complexity, e.g., a Zimbabwean community influenced by Crowdy that gradually shifted toward more normative Jewish practice, framing its descent as "spiritual if not genetic."

This book is not attacking every Black person who loves the Torah or identifies with Israel. It is confronting the strand that turns ethnicity into a saving category, makes hatred a virtue, and treats the gospel as insufficient unless it is "racially coded."

**Why Origins Matter (and Why This Is Not an Insult)**

A doctrine can be emotionally meaningful even if its historical scaffolding collapses; however, once a movement insists that its identity claim is not merely symbolic. However, the controlling key to Scripture is often asserted to be that salvation, divine favor, and prophetic fulfillment depend on it. The historical claim becomes a theological cornerstone. At that point, examining origins is not optional. It is basic intellectual and spiritual due diligence.

Christianity itself models this kind of honesty. Paul argues that the gospel stands or falls on historical events (1 Cor. 15:1–8).[14] That does not mean every Christian doctrine is "history-only"; rather, when a claim is presented as factual and foundational, it must be examined.

---

[14] May, Herbert G., 1943. "Archaeological News and Views: The Ten Lost Tribes", The Biblical Archaeologist(3), 6:55-60. https://doi.org/10.2307/3209244;

Mohamed, Hani Abdirachid, 2023. "African Civilization: From Ancient Kingdoms to Modern Societies", International Journal of Social Science and Human Research(06), 06. https://doi.org/10.47191/ijsshr/v6-i6-11;

Miller, Michael T., 2019. "Black Judaism(s) and the Hebrew Israelites", Religion Compass(11), 13. https://doi.org/10.1111/rec3.12346

This is where many extremist BHI strands are vulnerable: their confident rhetoric often depends on a storyline that claims to reach back into antiquity, but the documentary trail repeatedly lands us in modern American religious history visions, new congregations, and identity reconstruction under the violence of Jim Crow and its aftermath.

## A Note on "Black Suffering" and the Temptation to Overcorrect

It is possible to critique BHI exclusivism without denying the reality that has contributed to its psychological appeal. In fact, the book's sub-theme ("Doctrine of Devils") becomes sharper when you acknowledge the very human entry-point:

- Oppression creates a craving for meaning.

- Meaning-seeking can produce both healing and distortion.

- Distortion becomes "doctrine of devils" when it replaces the gospel with pride, hatred, and a counterfeit basis for righteousness.

So, this chapter should land with a tone that describes the following: The tragedy is not that wounded people reached for the Exodus story.

The tragedy is when a true story of God's deliverance is turned into a tool for racial supremacy, a denial of neighbor-love, and a denial of Christ's sufficient work.

## Closing Chapter 1 with a Clear Thesis Statement

Several points need to be understood from a historical perspective when discussing the fallacies of the BHI doctrine:

- It establishes that the modern BHI movement's recognizable forms emerge in late 1800s / early 1900s America (Cherry, Crowdy, and related currents).

- It establishes that many groups grew as identity-repair movements in response to slavery, segregation, and displacement, frequently drawing power from bondage-and-deliverance narratives.

- It does not establish a universal ancient Israelite genealogy for African Americans.

- It does not justify turning lineage into a new "law" that competes with the cross.

Having located the movement historically, we turn to the interpretive moves that make its claims appear "biblical."

# Chapter 2: Covenant Identity: What "Israel" Means Biblically

## Israel in the Old Testament: Covenant, Not Modern Race

In the Hebrew Bible, "Israel" is first a covenant people formed by God's election and promise (Gen. 12:1–3; Exod. 19:4–6).[15] Tribal identity mattered, but it was never identical with modern racial categories. Israelites themselves were a mixed population in the ancient Near East, and Israel repeatedly absorbed outsiders through covenant allegiance (e.g., Rahab in Josh. 6; Ruth in Ruth 1–4).

Because covenant is central, the prophets can both affirm Israel's election and condemn Israel's presumption. Election is never a permission slip for superiority; it is a summons to holiness and mission (Isa. 42:6; Amos 3:1–2).

When the Bible first names "Israel," it does not present a modern racial category. It presents a covenant people, a community brought into existence by God's promise, God's call, and God's binding relationship. Israel begins with an election and an oath, not with a sociology of skin tones. God calls Abram, promises him offspring, land, and a mission that extends beyond his own household: "in you all the families of the earth shall be blessed" (Gen. 12:1–3). Israel's identity is therefore never meant to terminate in Israel's self-glory; it is meant to serve God's redemptive purposes for the nations.

By the time Israel becomes a nation at Sinai, that covenant identity is stated explicitly: "You have seen what I did to the Egyptians… Now therefore, if you will indeed obey my voice and keep my covenant, you shall be my treasured possession… and you shall be to me a kingdom of priests

---

[15] Miller, Michael T., 2019. "Black Judaism(s) and the Hebrew Israelites", Religion Compass(11), 13. https://doi.org/10.1111/rec3.12346

and a holy nation" (Exod. 19:4–6). Notice the logic: belonging is covenantal, and covenantal belonging carries an ethical and missional calling to priesthood and holiness rather than a license to boast.

## Tribal reality without racial anachronism

Yes, the Israelite tribes, genealogies, and inheritance boundaries are included. The Old Testament is not embarrassed by kinship language. However, it is a mistake and an anachronism to treat ancient tribal identity as identical to modern "race," as if "Israelite" functions like a contemporary biological taxonomy. Ancient Near Eastern peoples intermarried, migrated, and absorbed outsiders through treaties, war, commerce, and adoption. Israel's Scriptures assume such an ancient world without flattening identity into modern categories.

Consider the following:

- Tribal identity mattered, but it was not a scientific "race."
- Covenant membership mattered most, and covenant membership repeatedly welcomed "outsiders" who pledged allegiance to Israel's God.

## Covenant incorporation: Israel repeatedly absorbs outsiders

This is not a minor detail; it is a built-in feature of the story.

Rahab, a Canaanite woman, entrusts herself to Israel's God, is spared, and is incorporated into Israel's life (Josh. 2; 6).

Ruth is a Moabite who binds herself to Yahweh and to Israel: "Your people shall be my people, and your God my God" (Ruth 1:16). Ruth becomes an ancestor in the Davidic line (Ruth 4), which means that Israel's royal story itself bears witness: faithful covenantal allegiance matters profoundly in the Bible's own self-understanding.[16]

---

[16] "Archaeological Perspective of the Lost Tribes of Israel," *The Biblical Archaeologist* 6, no. 3 (September 1943): 57–64.

This is precisely why serious biblical scholarship often points to Ruth as a built-in corrective to ethno-superiority claims. One archaeology-focused critique of "Lost Israel" mythmaking even highlights the "universalism" found in Isaiah's later chapters, the book of Ruth, and the New Testament as more central indicators of biblical integrity than speculative ethnic theories.[17]

## Election is not a permission slip; prophetic theology destroys presumption

A covenant doctrine that becomes a source of superiority is not "biblical Israel"; it is Israel's constant temptation, and the prophets confront it head-on.

Isaiah calls Israel to be "a light for the nations" (Isa. 42:6). That statement alone rebukes any inward-curving nationalism that regards Israel as an end in itself rather than an instrument of God's mercy.

Amos delivers one of the sharpest blows to ethnic presumption: Israel's election brings responsibility, not immunity. "You only have I known… therefore I will punish you…" (Amos 3:1–2). Election heightens accountability.

Biblically, the covenant confers identity but also imposes ethical demands. When Israel breaks the covenant, the prophets do not say, "Your bloodline guarantees your standing." They say, "Return. Repent. Covenant faithfulness matters." This is why any modern teaching that makes "Israel" a superiority badge is not simply mistaken; it is repeating the very sin the prophets condemned.

## "Israel" as a theological identity, not a racial weapon

Because covenant is central, "Israel" functions in Scripture as a theological reality: a people called by God, bound to God, disciplined by

---

[17] Gelston, Anthony. "Universalism in Second Isaiah." The journal of theological studies 43.2 (1992): 377-398.

God, and used by God. That is precisely why "Israelite" can never become a weapon to demean others while still claiming biblical legitimacy. The Bible's storyline does not support a gospel of racial elevation. It supports a covenant of holy calling and mercy centered on real historical Israel, with the nations in view from the beginning.

## The New Testament: One People of God in Christ

The New Testament does not erase Israel's story; it fulfills it in the Messiah. Jesus is the true Israelite who embodies the covenant (Matt. 2:15). In him, Gentiles are brought near not by becoming ethnic Jews, but by union with Christ (Eph. 2:11–22).

The New Testament does not erase Israel; it fulfills Israel's story in the Messiah and then extends the covenant blessing to the nations, as the Old Testament already anticipated.

### Jesus as "true Israel" and covenant fulfillment

Matthew's Gospel explicitly frames Jesus's early life in Israel-shaped terms: "Out of Egypt I called my son" (Matt. 2:15), echoing Hosea 11:1, where "son" originally referred to Israel. Matthew is not claiming Jesus is a new ethnic group; he is claiming Jesus recapitulates and fulfills Israel's calling where Israel failed; the Messiah succeeds. Jesus embodies covenant faithfulness, true sonship, true obedience, and true mission.

This is significant to the argument because it re-centers identity:

- In the Old Testament, Israel is God's covenant people.
- In the New Testament, Jesus is the faithful Israelite and covenant mediator.

Therefore, participation in the covenant promise is now defined fundamentally by union with Christ, not by claims of ethnic pedigree.

### Ephesians 2: the dividing wall falls, covenant membership expands

Ephesians 2:11–22 is one of the clearest passages for dismantling race-based salvific claims. Paul addresses Gentiles outside Israel's covenants and says they were once "far off," but are now "brought near by the blood of Christ." The mechanism of nearness is not DNA; it is atonement. Christ creates "one new man" from Jew and Gentile, reconciling both to God through the cross.

So the gospel does not require Gentiles to become ethnically Jewish to be saved. Instead, it brings them into the covenant blessings through Christ. This is covenant theology reaching its intended destination: Abraham's promised blessing flowing to "all families of the earth."

**Galatians 3: ethnic superiority cannot be a standing before God**

Any teaching that makes salvation depend on ethnic pedigree contradicts the apostolic gospel: "There is neither Jew nor Greek … for you are all one in Christ Jesus" (Gal. 3:28). This does not deny cultural difference; it denies ethnic superiority as a basis for standing before God. Paul goes even further: "There is neither Jew nor Greek… for you are all one in Christ Jesus" (Gal. 3:28). Paul is not denying cultural differences or flattening history. He is denying that ethnicity establishes righteous standing before God.

If a movement teaches that salvation depends on being the "right" ethnicity, it collides with apostolic Christianity at the foundation point. The gospel announcement is that Christ is sufficient and that faith in him, expressed in repentance, allegiance, and new life, defines covenant membership.

**Paul's "Israel" language: consistent, careful, and anti-boast:**

Paul is often misread here, so this helps clarify his logic. Paul affirms the historical privileges given to Israel (Rom. 9:1–5). He also insists that covenant participation is not automatic merely by descent (Rom. 9:6–8). He teaches that Gentile believers are "grafted in" by faith and warns them against boasting (Rom. 11). He maintains hope for Israel's future while refusing a race-based gospel in the present.

In other words, Paul can honor Israel's story without turning it into a salvific bloodline system. He refuses both anti-Jewish erasure and ethnocentric replacement gospels.

**Where extremist BHI teaching goes wrong:**

At the level of basic biblical definition, extremist BHI theology typically misfires in two linked ways:

- It turns covenant identity into biological supremacy, often treating "Israel" as a modern racial category rather than a covenant people with ethical obligations and a redemptive mission.

- It treats pedigree as soteriology as if the gospel is incomplete without a specific ethnic claim.

That is not how Scripture defines Israel. Moreover, even outside biblical theology, scholarship on Hebrew Israelite identity formation notes that "Israel" language can function as a symbolic identity, a powerful narrative of dignity and liberation, without being an objectively demonstrable genealogical claim.[18] When symbolic identity is hardened into racial dogma and then used as a basis for boasting or exclusion, it becomes not a healing story but a counterfeit gospel engine. Symbolic identity is not the same as a historically demonstrable genealogy, and it cannot be allowed to replace the gospel's covenant logic of faith and grace.[19]

---

[18] Shapira, Anita. "The bible and Israeli identity." AJS review 28.1 (2004): 11-41.

[19] Miller, "Black Judaism(s) and the Hebrew Israelites," Religion Compass 13, no. 11 (2019): e12346.

# Chapter 3: Deuteronomy 28 and the Slave-Trade Claim

## Deuteronomy 28 in Context

*Deuteronomy 28:68 And the Lord shall bring thee into Egypt again with ships, by the way whereof I spake unto thee, Thou shalt see it no more again: and there ye shall be sold unto your enemies for bondmen and bondwomen, and no man shall buy you.*

BHI teachers frequently identify the transatlantic slave trade with Deuteronomy 28:68 and treat the chapter as a coded map of modern history. However, Deuteronomy 28 is a covenant document addressed to ancient Israel on the brink of entering Canaan. The blessings and curses function within the Mosaic covenant: obedience brings life in the land; rebellion brings exile.

The chapter's "futility curses" align with a broader ancient Near Eastern treaty pattern; they are not prophecies requiring a twenty-first-century decoding key.[20] Deuteronomy is one of the primary scriptures the self-proclaimed BHI uses and draws on for its teachings. They have taken the position that the curse of Deut. 28:64 and 68 state, "the Lord shall scatter thee among all people, from the one end of the earth even unto the other…, the LORD shall bring thee into Egypt again with ships, " which is why the true Israelites were sold into slavery through the Trans-Atlantic Slave Trade throughout the Caribbean Islands and America. However, there are many problems with using Deuteronomy 28, and we will discuss the first problem in this chapter.

---

[20] Morrow, William S. "Ancient Near Eastern Treaties/Loyalty Oaths and Biblical Law." The Oxford Handbook of Biblical Law. Oxford University Press, 2019. 319.

## Exile, Restoration, and the Limits of Proof-Texting

Israel experienced covenant curses: Assyrian and Babylonian invasions, sieges, famine, deportations, and captivity (2 Kings 17; 25). When Scripture later speaks of restoration, it does so through the lens of the historical return from exile to the land, to covenant faithfulness, and ultimately to the coming of the Messiah.

To claim that Deuteronomy 28 uniquely predicts the transatlantic slave trade requires ignoring that the Bible itself already applies these curses to ancient Israel's exiles. It also requires treating a single verse as a universal template while disregarding its covenantal setting. The first problem of using Deuteronomy 28 is that it mentions they will return to Egypt by ships; however, Egypt could be used symbolically, but if this is literal, then what was warned as the punishment for disobeying GOD in Deuteronomy 28 did not happen due to the abolishment of the law, which is explained later in this chapter.

Another problem with using Deuteronomy 28 as an explanation for Hebrew Israelites coming to the Americas is that, in scripture, we already see a possible fulfillment of Deuteronomy 28 when the Assyrians captured the Northern Kingdom of Israel in 1 Kings chapter 17, and the Babylonians captured the Southern Kingdom of Israel in 2 Kings chapter 25. Through these enslavements, there were mass deportations of Israelites throughout the known world, and this is why, when they came out of captivity, many had to travel from far distances to take part in the High Holy Days or the Feast of Israel in Jerusalem. This is the very explanation of why, on the day of Pentecost, there were Jews from many nations who spoke different languages. Some scholars even believe that the Roman captivity of the Jews in 70 AD also played a major part in the Jews

being transported throughout the known world at the time, because slavery was a major business and component of the economy under Roman rule, and they used ships to enslave people and trade them throughout the world.

## The Trans-Atlantic Slave Trade Was Not the Fulfillment of Deut. 28

The transatlantic slave trade was a moral catastrophe and a profound sin against human beings made in God's image (Gen. 1:26–27). Scripture condemns man-stealing (Exod. 21:16; 1 Tim. 1:10). We do not need to force African American history into Deuteronomy 28 to speak biblically against slavery; the Bible already speaks clearly.

The term "four corners" is also problematic because it is used in the Bible as an idiom and should not be taken literally; it refers to the furthest reaches of the world, alluding to the extremity to which GOD will scatter the children of Israel. The phrase is figurative and does not indicate direction (north, south, east, or west). If it were literal, the four corners of the world would include South America, North America, Asia, and Africa; however, the trans-Atlantic slave trade only covered the Caribbean Islands, the Americas, and Europe, which is not the four corners of the earth. The truth is evident that Africans were sold into slavery throughout many areas of the world, but to say they were scattered throughout the four corners of the world in a literal sense is a far stretch!

See the Transatlantic Map on the next page:

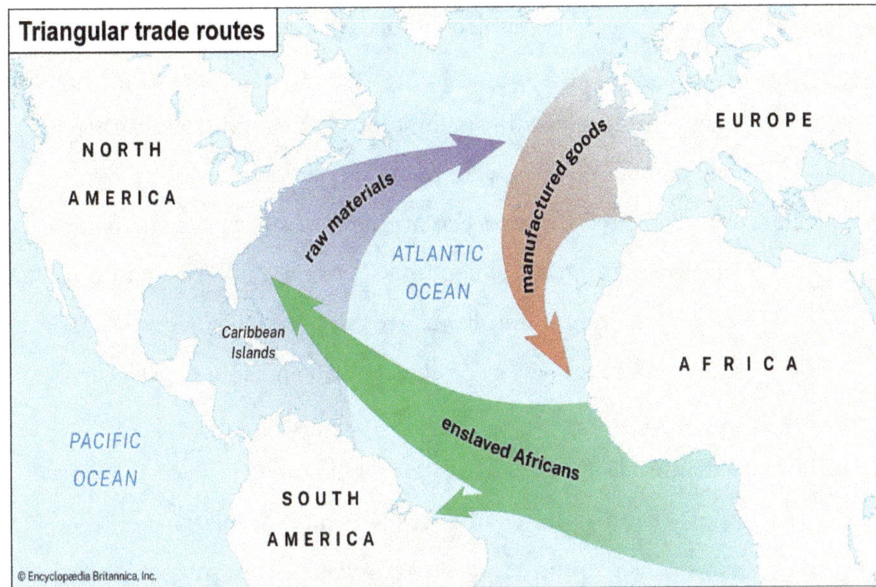



Source: "Transatlantic Slave Trade | History, Time Period, Causes, Effects, & Facts | Encyclopedia Britannica."

As the diagram shows, the slave trade did not send the Africans to the four corners of the world but only to the Americas, the Caribbean Islands, and some to Europe.

Slavery was big business way before the African Americans were shipped across to the Western world. Many rulers throughout history, including those of the Persian empires, used ships to transport enslaved people they acquired through the conquest of neighboring countries. For example, Alexander the Great conquered more of the known world than almost any ruler, enslaved many peoples, and transported his slaves by ship. He even conquered a province in Egypt and named it Alexandria. How is it that the self-proclaimed BHI has staked a claim that the warning that the LORD gave in Deuteronomy 28 was fulfilled when the West Africans were put into slavery? If this is the case, many races can claim to be the true Hebrew Israelites of the Bible, as will be demonstrated later in this book. During the time of the trans-Atlantic slave trade, several other nations, races, and ethnicities were also subjected to slavery and transported to different countries:

1.  Slavs and Iranians: From antiquity to the 19th century, Slavic and Iranian peoples were frequently enslaved.
2.  Sub-Saharan Africans: Enslavement of sub-Saharan Africans occurred from the 1st century CE to the mid-20th century.
3.  Germanic, Celtic, and Romance peoples: During the Viking era, these groups were often captured and sold into slavery.

The transatlantic slave trade, which predominantly involved the forced transportation of Africans to the Americas, was not an isolated phenomenon. Various nations, races, and ethnicities were subjected to enslavement during this period. The complexity of the slave trade is underscored by the involvement of multiple regions and ethnic groups, each contributing to the broader narrative of human trafficking.

Firstly, the African continent was a significant source of enslaved individuals, with various ethnic groups being captured and sold into slavery. Regions such as the Congo and Angola were particularly noted for their contributions to the transatlantic slave trade, as highlighted by those who discuss the genetic origins of liberated Africans on Saint Helena, linking them to these regions. Historical records indicate that trade routes shifted over time, reflecting changes in demand and supply dynamics within the slave trade (Sandoval-Velasco et al., 2019).[21] Moreover, the impact of the slave trade on local African societies was profound, leading to political fragmentation and altered kinship structures, as noted by.[22] The export of enslaved people not only depleted local populations but also transformed

---

[21] Sandoval-Velasco, Marcela, et al. "The genetic origins of Saint Helena's liberated Africans." BioRxiv (2019): 787515.

[22] Obikili, Nonso. "The trans-Atlantic slave trade and local political fragmentation in Africa." The Economic History Review 69.4 (2016): 1157-1177.

social structures, thereby increasing ethnic heterogeneity across the continent, as discussed by Whatley and Gillezeau.[23]

In addition to Africans, other groups were also subjected to enslavement. The indigenous populations of the Americas faced significant enslavement during the early colonial period, particularly in regions like the Caribbean and South America. The Spanish and Portuguese colonizers often enslaved local indigenous peoples to work in mines and plantations, a practice that predated the large-scale importation of enslaved Africans.[24] This early form of slavery laid the groundwork for the subsequent reliance on African slaves as indigenous populations dwindled due to disease and harsh labor conditions.

Furthermore, the transatlantic slave trade was not the only slave trade occurring during this period. The Arab slave trade, which predated and continued alongside the transatlantic trade, involved the capture and transportation of Africans to various parts of the Middle East and North Africa. This trade primarily targeted ethnic groups across Africa, including those in East Africa and the Sahel, and significantly influenced the demographic and cultural landscapes of these regions.[25] The interplay between these different slave trades highlights a broader context of human trafficking that transcended geographical boundaries.

Moreover, the dynamics of slavery were not limited to racial or ethnic lines; women and children were particularly vulnerable to enslavement. The gendered nature of the slave trade often resulted in women being exploited for domestic labor and sexual slavery, a trend that has historical roots in

---

[23] Whatley, Warren, and Rob Gillezeau. "The slave trade and ethnic stratification in Africa." Understanding African Poverty over the Lounge Durée Conference, Accra. 2010.

[24] Monteiro, John M. Blacks of the land: Indian slavery, settler society, and the Portuguese colonial enterprise in South America. Vol. 112. Cambridge University Press, 2018.

[25] Austen, Ralph A. Trans-Saharan Africa in world history. Oxford University Press, 2010.

various forms of servitude across cultures.[26] The implications of this gendered exploitation continue to resonate in contemporary discussions about slavery and human trafficking.

The transatlantic slave trade was part of a larger tapestry of human enslavement that included various nations, races, and ethnicities. The interconnectedness of these different forms of slavery illustrates the complexity of human trafficking throughout history, revealing a legacy that has shaped social, political, and economic structures across the globe.

## An Abolished Law

The second problem with Deuteronomy 28 is that it was part of the Old Covenant. A covenant is a legally binding contract between two parties. God and Israel were in a covenant, and Deuteronomy outlined its conditions. This is a significant problem in using Deuteronomy 28 to describe how the Israelites were sold into slavery in the Trans-Atlantic Slave Trade that started in the 17th century.

*Hebrews 12:24 states, "And to Jesus the mediator of the new covenant, and to the blood of sprinkling, that speaketh better things than that of Abel." (KJV)*

The new covenant ushered in a different way that the LORD dealt with his people. There was a new contract, and with it, the old contract was abolished! This presents a significant legal issue. The question needs to be asked, "Doth God pervert judgment? or doth the Almighty pervert justice (Job 8:3, KJV)?"

---

[26] West, Emily, and Erin Shearer. ": Fertility control, shared nurturing, and dual exploitation: the lives of enslaved mothers in the antebellum United States." Motherhood, Childlessness, and the Care of Children in Atlantic Slave Societies. Routledge, 2020. 117-131.

This question must be answered because it is illegal to breach a legally binding contract by invoking a clause from a contract that has been annulled or abolished.

*Galatians 3:13 Christ hath redeemed us from the curse of the law, being made a curse for us: for it is written, Cursed is every one that hangeth on a tree: (KJV)*

The curse of Deuteronomy 28 was abolished in A.D. 29, the Year of Our Lord, because it was part of a law that was only in effect during the Old Covenant. Furthermore, Paul stated, blotting out the handwriting of ordinances that was against us, which was contrary to us, and took it out of the way, nailing it to his cross (Col. 2:14, KJV).

"God is a just judge (Ps. 7:11, NET)," so why would he abolish a law and then wait one thousand and seven hundred plus years to break his own law and violate the covenant that he created to punish his people that he redeemed from the curse he established thousands of years prior! "Does God pervert justice? Alternatively, does the Almighty pervert what is right?" (Job 8:3, KJV) By the seventeenth century, the statutes of limitations had run out, and the perpetrators of the crime could no longer be prosecuted because the atonement of the Lord had been accomplished and grace had been ushered in. Even in the secular court of law in modern times, a judge must abide by current laws. I do not care what the defendant has done; the judge cannot invoke an old law that has been abolished just to punish the criminal more severely than current law allows. In other words, if I write a will for my children and state that I will leave all of my children a million dollars, and then before I die, I annul my will and change it to say that I was going to give all of my money to a charity instead. No matter how much my children may want the lawyer to execute my first will, the lawyer is required by law to execute my last will.

The major problem of Deuteronomy 28 is that the self-proclaimed BHI misuses it, and this misinterpretation has caused many people to be "tossed to and fro with every wind of doctrine" (Eph. 4:14, KJV). The false doctrine of the cultish group has hung its hat and set its foundation on Deuteronomy 28 and has been using it incorrectly due to their lack of knowledge of the Holy Scriptures. The scripture must be rightly divided, and to cherry-pick a scripture to start a movement out of racial radicalism is a great irrelevance to the Holy Scriptures.

# Chapter 4: The "Lost Tribes" Myth: History and Theology

## What Happened to the Northern Tribes?

The label "Ten Lost Tribes" is a popular myth, but historians and archaeologists caution against the idea of a total, mysterious disappearance.[27] Ancient deportations were real, yet they involved a fraction of the population and did not create a hidden global diaspora that can be traced to any modern nation by wordplay or folk etymology.[28]

H. G. May summarizes the scholarly consensus of his day: the "ten tribes" were never deported as a whole, many remained in the land, and the surviving populations intermingled with later communities (including what became the Samaritans). The fantasy of locating "lost Israel" is typically driven by desire rather than evidence.[29]

In this section, we must address this fallacy because it is evident that there were twelve tribes of Israel in the Bible. When I received literature from the self-proclaimed BHI, I was given a handout that demonstrates the confusion among most believers in this heresy. This handout describes how different ethnic groups represented different tribes of Israel. Also, some groups of the self-proclaimed Hebrew Israelites proclaim that all black people were the original Hebrew people and would stake the claim that the awakening has come to pass, where the black race would come to realize who they really are. If the black race is waking up to who they are, then I want to raise the question of why they are the only people who are waking up to this claim, and not the Native Americans, the Asians, the Indians, and

---

[27] Gow, A. "The Red Jews: Antisemitism in an Apocalyptic Age, 1200-1600". The American Historical Review, 1996.

[28] Younger, K. Lawson. "The deportations of the Israelites." Journal of Biblical Literature 117.2 (1998): 201-227.

[29] May, Herbert G., 1943. "Archaeological News and Views: The Ten Lost Tribes", The Biblical Archaeologist(3), 6:55-60. https://doi.org/10.2307/3209244

many other races that some self-proclaimed Hebrew Israelites claim to represent the other tribes. These claims cannot be validated, and throughout history, there have been many such claims. Which we will examine later in this chapter, but first, let us examine Judges 3:5-6.

"And the children of Israel dwelt among the Canaanites, Hittites, and Amorites, and Perizzites, and Hivites, and Jebusites: 6 And they took their daughters to be their wives, and gave their daughters to their sons, and served their gods" (Jdg. 3:5-6 KJV).

In this text, we see that the children of Israel dwelt among several nations, most notably those descended from Ham. They intermingled as they had throughout their history, even though the LORD had instructed them not to. With this in mind, the children of Israel were sprinkled among many nations, just as the claims of the Lemba people and the

Tower of Babel of Information: Almost every race has claimed to be the original Hebrews or the lost Tribes of Israel. The BHI comprises various sects, with some claiming to be the Tribe of Judah, others the original Hebrews, and still others the ten lost Tribes of Israel. All three are totally different constructs because you cannot be the Tribe of Judah and still be the ten lost Tribes of Israel. For one thing, the ten lost Tribes were not inclusive of Judah but were part of the northern Kingdom in Samaria. Judah occupied the southern kingdom with the tribe of Benjamin, so you are either one or the other. Secondly, the ten lost Tribes are mythical, and the Bible never validates that claim. Lastly, Judah remained in Palestine throughout the Roman period, beyond the 1st century A.D. (Anno Domini, the year after the Death of our LORD).

The history of various racial and ethnic groups claiming to be the original Hebrew Israelites is a complex narrative spanning centuries and encompassing diverse cultural, religious, and political contexts. The notion of Israelite identity has evolved significantly, influenced by historical events, archaeological findings, and sociopolitical movements.

From biblical times, the identity of the Israelites has been a subject of extensive scholarly debate. Tobolowsky's work, "The Myth of the Twelve Tribes of Israel," posits that claims to an Israelite identity are not merely historical artifacts but ongoing phenomena that have adapted over time. He emphasizes how the biblical accounts serve as a framework for constructing various visions of Israel, allowing different groups to assert their connection to the ancient Israelites.[30] This adaptability of identity is further supported by Whitelam, who discusses the shifting paradigms in the study of Israelite history, highlighting how archaeological and textual analyses have reshaped our understanding of who the Israelites were and how diverse groups have claimed their identity throughout history.[31]

In the modern context, the African Hebrew Israelites represent a significant movement that emerged in the 20th century, particularly during the Civil Rights and Black Power movements. This group asserts that contemporary Black individuals are the direct descendants of ancient Israelites, a claim central to their religious and cultural identity.[32] This assertion is part of a broader trend in which various ethnic groups, including those in Ethiopia, have claimed Israelite ancestry, often linking their historical narratives to biblical figures such as King Solomon and the Queen of Sheba. The Ethiopian Orthodox Church, for instance, has a long-standing tradition of identifying with Israelite heritage, which has been integral to its national identity.[33]

---

[30] Tobolowsky, Andrew, 2022. "The Myth of the Twelve Tribes of Israel",. https://doi.org/10.1017/9781009091435

[31] Whitelam, Keith W., 2000. "The History of Israel: Foundations of Israel", Text in Context:376-402. https://doi.org/10.1093/0198263910.003.0014

[32] Dorman, Jacob S. Chosen People: The Rise of American Black Israelite Religions. Oxford University Press, 2012.

[33] Kaplan, Steven. "Genealogies and gene-ideologies: The legitimacy of the Beta Israel (Falasha)." Social identities 12.4 (2006): 447-455.

The historical context of Jewish identity itself further complicates the interplay of race and identity. The term "Jewish" often refers to religious adherence, while "Hebrew" and "Israelite" can denote ethnic origins. This distinction has led to various groups, including Ashkenazi Jews, being labeled as impostors by some factions who claim a more authentic connection to the ancient Israelites.[34] This discourse reflects broader themes of racial identity and historical legitimacy that have permeated discussions about who can rightfully claim the Israelite legacy.

Moreover, scholarly discourse on the historicity of the Hebrew Bible and its narratives has also shaped these claims. The Documentary Hypothesis, articulated by scholars such as Wellhausen, posits that the biblical texts were compiled from various sources, with implications for understanding the historical claims of different groups.[35] This critical approach allows for a nuanced examination of how these texts have been used to construct identities over time.

The history of various racial and ethnic groups claiming to be the original Hebrew Israelites is marked by a dynamic interplay of historical narratives, religious beliefs, and sociopolitical movements. The ongoing reinterpretation of Israelite identity continues to shape the cultural landscapes of various communities, reflecting a rich tapestry of claims that are as diverse as the groups themselves.

## Why the "Lost Tribes" Myth Keeps Returning

The myth is attractive because it offers prestige and a sense of destiny. Across centuries, many groups, including Anglo-Israelites, some Native American theorists, and some African and Pacific communities, have claimed Israelite descent. Tudor Parfitt documents how religious and

---

[34] Smooha, Sammy. "Jewish ethnicity in Israel: Symbolic or real." Jews in Israel: Contemporary social and cultural patterns 1 (2004): 47-80.

[35] Wellhausen, Julius. "Documentary hypothesis."

political pressures repeatedly generate such claims, even when historical links are tenuous.[7]

The myth of the Lost Tribes of Israel has captivated diverse peoples throughout history, prompting many groups to claim descent from these tribes. This phenomenon can be traced to the biblical narrative, which describes the division of the ancient Kingdom of Israel into two parts: the northern kingdom, comprising ten tribes, and the southern kingdom of Judah, comprising the tribes of Judah and Benjamin, along with some Levites. The Assyrian conquest in 722 BCE led to the exile of the northern tribes, which subsequently became known as the "Lost Tribes."[36]

However, the book of James was written between A.D. 44 and A.D. 62, yet it was written to the twelve tribes of Israel during that time.

***James 1:1 James, a servant of God and of the Lord Jesus Christ, to the twelve tribes which are scattered abroad, greeting. KJV***

The question is: when did the tribes become lost? Most adherents of the lost tribes of Israel will date their loss centuries before James wrote his epistle.

The allure of the Lost Tribes myth lies in its potential to shape identity and confer cultural legitimacy. For instance, in Fiji, certain clans assert their descent from the Lost Tribes, a belief that gained prominence during political upheavals in the late 20th century.[37] This connection to a biblical heritage provides a sense of historical significance and belonging, particularly in contexts where indigenous identities are under threat. Similarly, in Papua New Guinea, a group of Gogodala-speaking villagers claimed descent from the Lost Tribes, reflecting local interest in biblical

---

[36] Dundon, Alison, 2015. "Babala and the Bible: Israel and a 'Messianic Church' in Papua New Guinea", Oceania(3), 85:327-341. https://doi.org/10.1002/ocea.5099

[37] Newland, Lynda, 2015. "The Lost Tribes of Israel – and the Genesis of Christianity in Fiji: Missionary Notions of Fijian Origin from 1835 to Cession and Beyond", Oceania(3), 85:256-270. https://doi.org/10.1002/ocea.5106

teachings as a framework for understanding their origins.[38] Such claims often reinforce community cohesion and provide a narrative of resilience in the face of colonial and postcolonial challenges.

The myth has also found resonance in the Americas, particularly during the 17th century when the Israelite-AmeriIndian theory emerged. Proponents like Thomas Thorowgood and Menasseh ben Israel posited that Native Americans were descendants of the Lost Tribes, a notion that intertwined with colonial ideologies and the quest for legitimacy in the New World.[39] This theory not only sought to explain the presence of indigenous peoples but also reflected the broader European fascination with biblical narratives as a means of justifying colonial expansion.[40]

Moreover, the appeal of the Lost Tribes myth extends to contemporary movements, such as among the Igbo people of Nigeria, who assert their identity as a Lost Tribe. This claim is often framed within the context of ethnonationalism and the quest for recognition in a postcolonial landscape.[41] Such assertions highlight the ongoing relevance of the Lost Tribes narrative in shaping modern identities and political aspirations.

The myth of the Lost Tribes of Israel has been appropriated by various races and ethnicities to assert identity, legitimacy, and historical continuity. This phenomenon illustrates the enduring power of biblical narratives in shaping cultural and political discourses across diverse contexts.

---

[38] Handman, Courtney, 2011. "Israelite Genealogies and Christian Commitment: The Limits of Language Ideologies in Guhu-Samane Christianity", Anthropological Quarterly(3), 84:655-677. https://doi.org/10.1353/anq.2011.0045

[39] Crome, Andrew, 2015. "Politics and Eschatology: Reassessing the Appeal of the "Jewish Indian" Theory in England and New England in the 1650s", Journal of Religious History(3), 40:326-346. https://doi.org/10.1111/1467-9809.12301

[40] Cogley, Richard W., 2007. ""Some Other Kinde of Being and Condition": The Controversy in Mid-Seventeenth-Century England over the Peopling of Ancient America", Journal of the History of Ideas(1), 68:35-56. https://doi.org/10.1353/jhi.2007.0003

[41] Ejiofor, Promise Frank, 2022. "Jewishness without Jews? Ontological Security, Ethnonationalism, and the Social Power of Analogical Reasoning in Postcolonial Nigeria", Nationalities Papers:1-29. https://doi.org/10.1017/nps.2022.70

## List of Groups that Claim Descent From the Tribes of Israel

There are many BHI who believe that the Haitians are the true Levites. This belief is rooted in hypothetical reasoning. The BHI believes they are not using any Biblical rituals or systems of synagogue worship and are isolated from other nations, independent of certain Old Testament laws or commandments, until God brings them all back to Jerusalem to the third temple. This belief is not only that the Haitians but all Israelites will return to Jerusalem and have in captivity those who have put them in captivity. This is BHI's erroneous thought process. However, they are not the only group to claim Israelite lineage; several groups throughout history have made similar claims.

### *Pashtuns (Pakhtuns) of Afghanistan and Pakistan*

The Pashtuns are a predominantly Sunni Muslim Iranian people indigenous to Afghanistan and Pakistan who maintain a distinctive pre-Islamic code of conduct and identity known as Pashtunwali.[42] Although some Pashtun traditions and popular accounts claim descent from the "lost tribes" of Israel, historians note that this claim has not been demonstrated by firm historical evidence.[43] Modern references to the idea persist even among groups drawn from Pashtun tribal networks, including Taliban-linked milieus, without necessarily being treated as a central or testable historical claim.

A frequently cited example is the Pashto tribal name Yusef Zai, often glossed as "sons of Joseph."[44] Contemporary genetic literature is mixed: some studies are invoked to argue against an Israelite connection,

---

[42] Khan, Hameed Ullah, and Nasir Ahmed. "A genealogical study of the origin of Pashtuns." International conference on intelligent computing. Berlin, Heidelberg: Springer Berlin Heidelberg, 2013.

[43] Stanizai, Zaman. "Are Pashtuns the Lost Tribe of Israel?." (2023).

[44] Ibid.

while others are presented as suggestive of limited links, though popular summaries often overstate what genetic data can conclusively establish about ancient tribal identities. In the same vein, The Guardian reported that Israel intended to fund genetic research to evaluate a proposed Pashtun–Israelite connection, while acknowledging that definitive proof had not been found.[45]

### *Kurdish Jews*

Accounts within Kurdish Jewish folklore have sometimes described local Jewish communities as connected to the Ten Lost Tribes, a theme noted in modern reporting and reference works. Broader historical narratives also point to population movements and resettlements in the Near East following Assyrian imperial campaigns, which later communities sometimes linked rightly or wrongly to tribal origin stories.[46]

Tradition holds that Israelites of the tribe of Benjamin first arrived in the area of modern Kurdistan after the Assyrian conquest of the Kingdom of Israel during the 8th century BC; they were subsequently relocated to the Assyrian capital.[47] During the first century BC, the royal house of Adiabene, which, according to the Jewish historian Flavius Josephus, was ethnically Assyrian and whose capital was Erbil (Aramaic: Arbala; Kurdish: Hewlêr), was converted to Judaism.[48] King Monobazes,

---

[45] Aafreedi, Navras J. "Chapter Fourteen The Tradition of Israelite Descent Among The Pashtuns In India and Its Contemporary Ramifications." Africana Jewish Journeys: Studies in African Judaism (2018): 202.

[46] Ammann, Birgit. "The Kurdish Jewish communities: Lost forever." Religious minorities in Kurdistan: Beyond the mainstream (2014): 271-300.

[47] Aster, Shawn Zev. "Transmission of Neo-Assyrian Claims of Empire to Judah in the Late Eighth Century BCE." Hebrew Union College Annual, vol. 78, 2007, pp. 1-23.

[48] Rabin, Anthony. The Adiabene narrative in the Jewish Antiquities of Josephus. Diss. University of Oxford, 2017.

his queen Helena, and his son and successor, Izates, are recorded as the first proselytes.[49]

## *Kashmiri Jews*

A recurring theory holds that Kashmir has historical associations with Jews or Israelite migrants. Medieval scholar al-Bīrūnī is often cited in later discussions as mentioning the restricted admission of foreigners, "particularly Jews," into Kashmir in earlier times.  Later travelers and writers also speculated about perceived physical similarities between Kashmiris and Jews, though these claims are typically observational and not evidentiary.  Other writers note that surname parallels or surface-level resemblances do not establish ancestry and emphasize Indo-Aryan origins for Kashmiri Pandits rather than a Semitic lineage.[50]

## *Bene Israel*

The Bene Israel are a historic Jewish community in India (especially in Maharashtra and the Konkan region) whose traditions of origin include narratives of migration and extended periods of partial isolation from rabbinic centers.[51] Community memory also recounts a later "rediscovery" and instruction by Jewish figures associated with Cochin, often traditionally linked to David Rahabi, who encouraged a fuller alignment with normative Jewish practice.[52]

Scholarly discussion has sometimes linked the Bene Israel to "lost tribes" traditions, but modern treatments more commonly distinguish

---

[49] Marciak, Michał. "Izates and Helena of Adiabene: a study on literary traditions and history Date: 2012-11-20." (2012).

[50] Aafreedi, Navras Jaat. "Claimants of Israelite Descent in South Asia." The Journal of Indo-Judaic Studies 14 (2014).

[51] Elazar, Gideon, and Miriam Billig. "The Immigration and Strategic Assimilation of Bene Menashe: A Zomian Jewish Community in Israel." Asian Studies Review 49.2 (2025): 424-442.

[52] Fischel, Walter J. "Cochin in Jewish history: Prolegomena to a history of the Jews in India." Proceedings of the American Academy for Jewish Research. Vol. 30. American Academy for Jewish Research, 1962.

between communal origin stories and what can be demonstrated historically. Genetic research has been interpreted as consistent with Middle Eastern paternal ancestry alongside substantial local admixture, aligning with long-settlement models rather than proving descent from any specific ancient tribe. In Israel, disputes over personal-status issues eventually culminated in official recognition that the Bene Israel were "full Jews in every respect."[53]

## Bnei Menashe

Since the late twentieth century, some communities in Mizoram and Manipur have claimed descent from the Israelites (often identifying with the tribe of Manasseh) and have pursued Hebrew studies and Jewish practice. Following religious review processes, Israeli rabbinic authorities supported pathways for immigration contingent on formal conversion procedures.[54]

## Beta Israel of Ethiopia

Beta Israel (Ethiopian Jews) have been described historically under labels such as "Falashas," though the latter term is widely regarded as outdated. Within the community and among some scholars, one claim traces Beta Israel's ancestry to the tribe of Censored, while other traditions trace their origins to the Solomonic/Sheba narrative. Genetic studies have often been interpreted to show strong Ethiopian ancestry overall, with some work suggesting possible contributions from a smaller number of Jewish ancestors in late antiquity, claims that remain bounded by the limits

---

[53] Hodes, Joseph R. "The Bene Israel and the "Who Is a Jew" Controversy in Israel." Who is a Jew?: Reflections on History, Religion, and Culture (Studies in Jewish Civilization) (2014): 169-192.

[54] Samra, Myer. "The Benei Menashe: Choosing Judaism in North East India." The Journal of Indo-Judaic Studies 12 (2012): 45-57.

of genetic inference. Israeli rabbinic rulings in the 1970s recognized Beta Israel as Jewish, supporting large-scale immigration.[55]

Some members of the Beta Israel, as well as several Jewish scholars, believe they are descended from the lost Tribe of Dan rather than from the traditional story of descent from the Queen of Sheba. They have a tradition of being connected to Jerusalem. Early DNA studies indicated they were descended from Ethiopians. However, in the 21st century, new studies suggest they may descend from a few Jews who lived in the 4th or 5th century, possibly in Sudan.[56] The Beta Israel made contact with other Jewish communities in the late 20th century. In 1973, Rabbi Ovadia Yosef, then the Chief Sephardic Rabbi, based on the Radbaz and other accounts, ruled that the Beta Israel were Jews and should be brought to Israel; two years later, that opinion was confirmed by several other authorities who made similar rulings, including the Chief Ashkenazi Rabbi Shlomo Goren.[57]

## Igbo Jews

Some Igbo communities in Nigeria have advanced claims of descent from various Israelite tribes. Historical scholarship examining "origin" theories in colonial and postcolonial West African contexts cautions that such narratives often served political and social functions for the writers and institutions promoting them, rather than reflecting demonstrable ancient migrations.[58]

## Sefwi (House of Israel) in Ghana

A small community associated with the Sefwi in southwestern Ghana has practiced Sabbath observance, circumcision on the eighth day,

---

[55] Kaplan, Steven. "Genealogies and gene-ideologies: The legitimacy of the Beta Israel (Falasha)." Social identities 12.4 (2006): 447-455.

[56] Ibid.

[57] Kaplan, Steven. The Beta Israel (Falasha) in Ethiopia: from earliest times to the twentieth century. NYU Press, 1992.

[58] Uzukwu, E. Elochukwu. "Igbo world and ultimate reality and meaning." Ultimate Reality and Meaning 5.3 (1982): 188-209.

and other customs framed as Jewish and later organized as the "House of Israel."[59] Community narratives often trace renewed Jewish identification to visions reported by Aaron Ahotre Toakyirafa in the late 1970s, with some external interpretations attributing certain customs to historical contact routes (including possible North African or Iberian-Jewish movements via Morocco) rather than direct descent from a specific Israelite tribe.[60]

## Scythian/Cimmerian theories and British Israelism

British Israelism and related movements proposed that the lost tribes migrated into Eurasia and ultimately became the ancestors of later European peoples.[61] The tradition developed in Britain and later spread to the United States, where it was promoted in the twentieth century by figures such as Herbert W. Armstrong. Historians and critical scholars have generally rejected these arguments as methodologically weak and reliant on speculative correlations rather than credible historical evidence.[62]

## Native Americans

From the seventeenth century onward, some English writers argued that Indigenous peoples of the Americas descended from the Ten Lost Tribes.[63] Thomas Thorowgood's Ievves in America advanced this idea, while Hamon L'Estrange published a rebuttal challenging it. In the nineteenth century, Mordecai Manuel Noah also promoted a related thesis

---

[59] Salm, Steven J., and Toyin Falola. "Culture and customs of Ghana." (2002): 1-246.

[60] Levin, Ayala. Architecture and Development: Israeli Construction in Sub-Saharan Africa and the Settler Colonial Imagination, 1958-1973. 2022.

[61] Gamkrelidze, Thomas V., and Vjačeslav V. Ivanov. "The migrations of tribes speaking the Indo-European dialects from their original homeland in the Near East to their historical habitations in Eurasia." Soviet Studies in History 22.1-2 (1983): 53-95.

[62] Cottrell-Boyce, Aidan. Israelism in modern Britain. Routledge, 2020.

[63] Huddleston, Lee Eldridge. Origins of the American Indians: European Concepts, 1492-1729. Vol. 11. University of Texas Press, 2015.

in public discourse.[64] Modern historians treat these claims as products of colonial-era biblical frameworks and identity projects rather than conclusions grounded in archaeology or Indigenous histories.

## *Japanese*

A fringe tradition sometimes called the "Japanese–Jewish common ancestry" theory claimed that Japanese origins could be linked to the Israelites. One early proponent, Nicholas McLeod, attempted to correlate Japanese history and customs with biblical narratives in the nineteenth century.[65] Later writers describe such theories as part of a broader colonial-era impulse to interpret diverse cultures through biblical models. Genetic arguments are frequently cited as contradicting claims of close Israelite–Japanese ancestry, at least at any meaningful population scale.[66]

Some writers have speculated that the Japanese people may be the direct descendants of some of the Ten Lost Tribes. The spread of the fantasy of Israelite origin is a consistent feature of the Western colonial enterprise, where, in fact, we can trace the most remarkable evolution in the Pacific of an imagined Judaic past in Japan. As elsewhere in the world, the theory that aspects of the country were to be explained via an Israelite model was introduced by Western agents.[67]

In 1878, Scottish immigrant to Japan Nicholas McLeod self-published the Epitome of the Ancient History of Japan.

---

64 Cogley, Richard W. "" Some Other Kinde of Being and Condition": The Controversy in Mid-Seventeenth-Century England over the Peopling of Ancient America." Journal of the History of Ideas 68.1 (2007): 35-56.

65 McLeod, Nicholas C. "Practicing Pan-Africanism: West Indians and governance in Kwame Nkrumah's Ghana." (2020).

66 Egorova, Yulia. "The proof is in the genes? Jewish responses to DNA research." Culture and Religion 10.2 (2009): 159-175.

67 Bar-Yosef, Eitan. The Holy Land in English culture 1799-1917: Palestine and the question of Orientalism. OUP Oxford, 2005.

McLeod drew correlations between his observations of Japan and the fulfillment of biblical prophecy:[68] The civilized race of the Aa. Inus,[sic: read Ainus] the Tokugawa and the Machi No Hito of the large towns, by dwelling in the tent or tabernacle-shaped houses first erected by Jin Mu Tenno, have fulfilled Noah's prophecy regarding Japhet, "He shall dwell in the tents of Shem."

Jon Entine emphasizes that DNA evidence shows there are no genetic links between the Japanese and Israelite people.[69]

## Māori

Some early missionaries speculated that Māori origins might be connected to the Lost Tribes, an idea later discussed in New Zealand reference treatments of Māori origin theories.[70]

## Lemba

The Lemba of southern Africa have long maintained oral traditions that some of their ancestors were Jewish migrants (often associated with routes from Yemen) who intermarried locally while transmitting certain practices interpreted as Judaic.[71] Popular science coverage has highlighted genetic findings, sometimes presented as consistent with limited Near Eastern paternal ancestry in some Lemba lineages, while also emphasizing the complexity of translating genetic findings into claims about ancient Israelite tribes.[72]

---

[68] McLeod, Norman. Epitome of the ancient history of Japan. auther [sic] at the Rising Sun Office, 1878.

[69] Ibid.

[70] Salmond, Anne. "Maori epistemologies." Reason and morality. Routledge, 2003. 237-260.

[71] Buijs, Gina. "Black Jews in the Northern Province: a study of ethnic identity in South Africa." Ethnic and racial studies 21.4 (1998): 661-682.

[72] Goldschmidt, E., and T. Cohen. "Inter-ethnic mixture among the communities of Israel." Cold Spring Harbor Symposia on Quantitative Biology. Vol. 29. Cold Spring Harbor Laboratory Press, 1964.

# Chapter 5: Genealogy and "Proofs": What Counts as Evidence?

## Genealogy, Genetics, and the Limits of Modern Proof

Many BHI arguments rely on speculative "linguistics," misused DNA claims, or the assumption that shared customs prove direct descent.[73] Scholars warn that such methods are usually deductive: a desired conclusion is assumed, and then selective similarities are gathered to support it.

Modern genetic tools can sometimes illuminate population histories, but they cannot retroactively turn a modern ethnoracial label into an ancient tribal identity.[74] Genetic overlap can reflect trade, migration, and intermarriage across millennia. It is not a shortcut to biblical covenant status.

### Biblical Genealogies Do Not Work Like Street-Corner Charts

Scripture employs genealogies for theological purposes, such as messianic lineage, covenant continuity, and land inheritance, rather than to map modern racial categories onto biblical tribes. When the New Testament confronts genealogical obsession, it calls it "unprofitable and worthless" when used to stir division.

*Titus 3:9 states, "But avoid foolish controversies, genealogies, quarrels, and fights about the law, because they are useless and empty (NET)."*

*1 Timothy 1:3-4 also states, "As I urged you when I was leaving for Macedonia, stay on in Ephesus to instruct certain people not to*

---

[73] Imhoff, Sarah, and Hillary Kaell. "Lineage matters: DNA, race, and gene talk in Judaism and Messianic Judaism." Religion and American Culture 27.1 (2017): 95-127.

[74] Pickrell, Joseph K., and David Reich. "Toward a new history and geography of human genes informed by ancient DNA." Trends in Genetics 30.9 (2014): 377-389.

*spread false teachings, nor to occupy themselves with myths and interminable genealogies. Such things promote useless speculations rather than God's redemptive plan that operates by faith (NET)."*

We must recognize that the Bible condemns debate over genealogies because, as Paul informed Timothy and Titus, such debate is not part of the doctrine we are to teach; it is controversial, unedifying, unprofitable, and empty. It is extremely careless to stake a claim to the identity of an ancient people on subjective evidence. This is why Paul expresses the devices of subjects like this one as unprofitable and vain. Furthermore, no historical or genetic evidence exists to support that African Americans are physical descendants of the ancient Israelites.[75]

## Genealogies & Haplogroups

Nevertheless, let us look at genealogies and haplogroups instead of DNA because it will make more sense to look at the family tree of the Israelites and people groups that are related to them, because of all of the confusion that DNA can present when people do not understand it, especially when we all have DNA of different haplogroups within us. Even the children of Israel mixed with other races of people in their existence as a nation.

Genealogy is the tracing of a line of descent continuously from an ancestor. Haplogroups make identity much simpler and provide historical and Biblical evidence that the self-proclaimed BHI cannot be the original Hebrew Israelites. A haplogroup is a group of similar haplotypes that share a common ancestor with a single-nucleotide polymorphism mutation. With this in mind, we must understand that Abraham is the common ancestor of many Semitic races.

---

[75] Ostrer, H. "A genetic view of Jewish history". Nature Genetics, 2008.

The genealogy of Abraham: Father of the Israelites, a descendant of Shem (Genesis 11:10-26). Known as the patriarch of monotheistic faiths. Abraham was the son of Terah, who also fathered Nahor and Haran (Genesis 11:27). Abraham married Sarah (originally Sarai). He had Isaac, the promised child through the covenant God established with Abraham. Abraham also had a son, Ishmael, with his servant, Hagar, an Egyptian maidservant of Sarah. This makes Ishmael part Hebrew and part Egyptian. Ishmael was sent away and settled in the southern part of Israel, known as Beersheba and the Desert of Paran. It is important to note that Abraham came from pagan roots and a people who were likely Amorite or Aramean, generally identified as from the Sumerian city of Ur of the Chaldees in Southern Mesopotamia (modern-day Iraq), before he was considered a Hebrew. Abraham was part of an Amorite or Aramean culture; he came from a pagan, Akkadian-speaking, or Sumerian-influenced society before migrating west to Canaan. He was a native speaker of Akkadian or a related Semitic language in his early life.

Abraham's genealogy is as follows:

**From Abraham:**

- Son of **Terah**, who also fathered Nahor and Haran (Genesis 11:27).
- Married **Sarah** (originally Sarai) and had **Isaac** (through the covenant) and **Ishmael** (through Hagar).
- After Sarah's death, Abraham married **Keturah** (Genesis 25:1-4), who bore six additional sons: **Zimran, Jokshan, Medan, Midian, Ishbak, and Shuah**. These sons are ancestors of various tribes in Arabia and the surrounding regions.

**From Isaac:**

- **Isaac and Rebekah** had twins:
    - **Jacob**: Renamed Israel; father of the **12 tribes** (Genesis 35:22-26).
    - **Esau**: Ancestor of the **Edomites** (Genesis 36), who lived in Seir and intermarried with local Horites.

**From Jacob:**

- Jacob's 12 sons (listed earlier) became the heads of the tribes of Israel. The tribe of Levi became priests and did not receive land, while Joseph's lineage split into two tribes (Ephraim and Manasseh).

**Lot's Lineage:**

- Lot, Abraham's nephew, fathered two sons through his daughters (Genesis 19:30-38):
    - **Moab**: Ancestor of the Moabites.
    - **Ben-Ammi**: Ancestor of the Ammonites.
- These nations had both adversarial and occasional cooperative interactions with Israel throughout history.

**From Ishmael:**

- Ishmael had 12 sons (Genesis 25:13-16) who became leaders of Arab tribes, including **Nebaioth** and **Kedar**, prominent in Arab genealogies.

**From Keturah:**

- Keturah's children were ancestors of various Arabian tribes. For example:

- o **Midian**: Associated with the Midianites, mentioned in the story of Moses (Exodus 2:15-21).

- o **Shuah**: Possibly linked to a tribe in the Syrian desert.

If we traced the genealogy of Abraham, we would find several races that we call his descendants, but because he is the common ancestor, they are all in the same haplogroup. Let us observe Abraham's family tree below, starting with his father Terah:

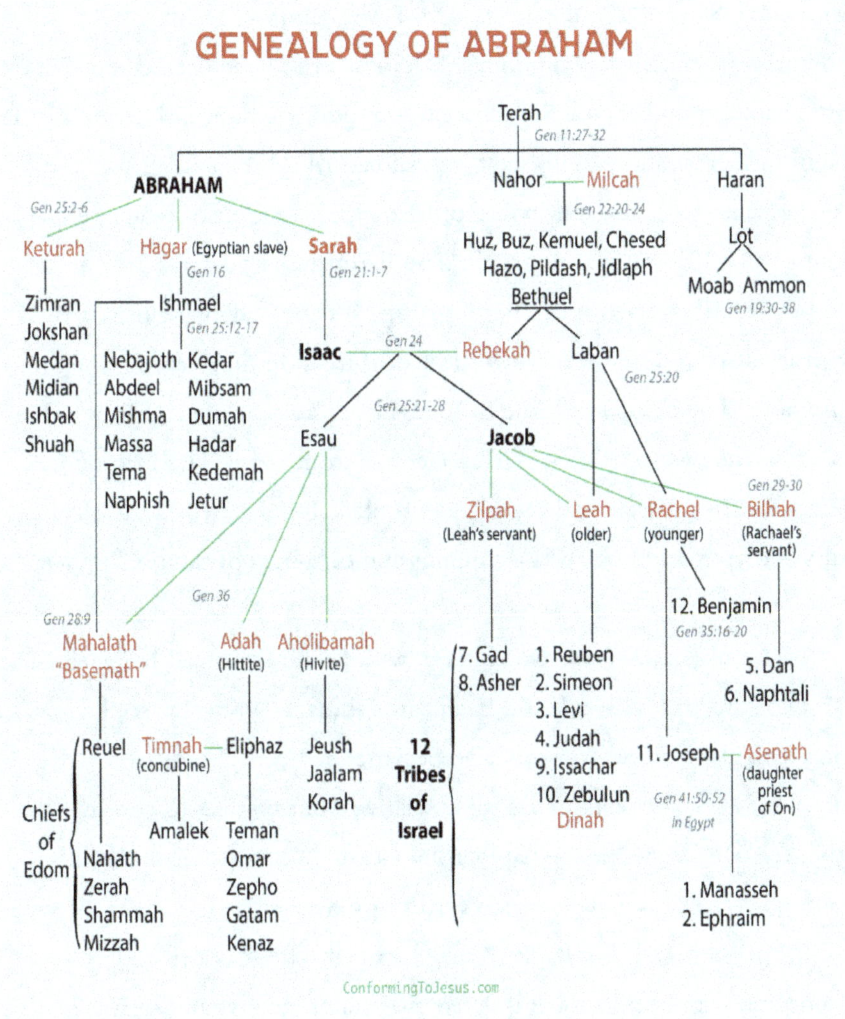



Source: Conformingtojesus.com | Chart of the Genealogy Of Abraham | Abraham's Family Tree.

Notice the names Ishmael, Moab, Ammon, Edom, and Israel on the chart. This indicates that, through the genealogy of Abraham and his two sons, Ishmael and Isaac, the Ishmaelites emerged as a nation. Around the same time, Abraham's nephew Lot had two sons, Moab and Ben-ammi, who became the Moabites and the Ammonites. Then Abraham's son, Isaac, had two sons, Esau and Jacob, from whom the Edomites and the Israelites descended. So, through the genealogy of Abraham, we see that the Ishmaelites, Moabites, Ammonites, Edomites, and Israelites belong to the same haplogroup because they share a common ancestor, Terah. Now, this might be a great shock to the self-proclaimed BHI because of their disdain for the white race, and they will express their intolerance of white people by calling them Edomites as an insult. **The Edomites and Israelites are the closest relatives within the haplogroup, yet the self-proclaimed BHI express strong disdain toward the Edomites, demonstrating** their ignorance. The Edomites came from Esau, the twin brother of Jacob, the father of the twelve tribes of Israel. Jacob is from Israel. The Edomites descended from Esau, and the Bible describes him as "red, all over like a hairy garment; and Esau was a cunning hunter, a man of the field" (Gen. 25:25,27, KJV).

Abraham fathered two children with Sarah: Isaac and Ishmael. Isaac had two sons named Jacob and Esau, and Ishmael had twelve sons. Isaac's son Jacob also had twelve sons who became the twelve heads of the twelve tribes of Israel. We will discuss these relatives, but first, let us consider their other relatives to define the haplogroup clearly. When Abraham left his home to go to a place where the LORD would show him, he took his wife and his nephew Lot. Lot had two daughters who fled Sodom and Gomorrah with him to some isolated mountains, and when Lot was in a state of impairment, his daughters considered their own survival and lay with their father to have children. From these children came the Moabites and the Ammonites. Around the same time that the Ishmaelite, Moabite, and Ammonite nations were forming, the nation of Israel was emerging; these nations predate Israel, yet remain related.

Another important point is that Abraham and many other Hebrew men often took wives or concubines from other nations, which led to the presence of Y chromosomes in populations that were not originally of Hebrew descent. Abraham had an Egyptian wife; Esau had a Hittite, Egyptian, and a Hivite wife; Joseph had an Egyptian wife; and the children of Israel had wives from Canaan. All of these wives came from outside their haplogroups and had children with them. Even King Solomon is said to have fathered a child with the Queen of Sheba. The Y chromosome could very well appear in DNA from other haplogroups, but this does not mean that their dominant genotype is of Jewish/Hebrew origin.

## Genetic Context and Haplogroups

- Haplogroup J (J1 and J2):
    - J1: Strongly linked to Semitic-speaking populations, including Arabs and Jews. Associated with Abraham's lineage due to its prevalence among Jewish Kohanim (priests), a lineage traditionally traced to Aaron, Moses' brother.
    - J2: Found in populations around the Mediterranean and associated with ancient Levantine civilizations like the Phoenicians and Canaanites.
- Haplogroup E1b1b:
    - Also found among Jewish populations, particularly Sephardic Jews. This haplogroup is common in North

African populations and suggests admixture during the diaspora and interactions with surrounding nations.

- Genetic Diversity of Descendants:

    The genetic makeup of modern Jews reflects a mixture of Middle Eastern origins and diaspora admixture with European, North African, and other regional groups.

The key thing to understand is that the children of Israel were a family that began with Abraham's obedience to follow God and had a son named Isaac, who had two sons named Jacob and Esau. Jacob, whose name God changed to Israel, had twelve sons, and their families continued to grow and came to be known as the Jewish people, or Israelite/Hebrew people. There were already nations that occupied much of the known world at that time and predated the family of the Israelites. The children of Israel are the covenant people of God. Still, before Abraham, there were many people considered God's people who were not from the twelve families descended from Jacob's twelve sons. Namely, Adam, Abel, Seth, Enosh, Enoch, Methuselah, Noah, Shem, Eber, and Melchizedek are a short list of people mentioned in the Bible as God's people who were not Hebrew. We cannot forget about Job, whom God describes as his servant in the book of Job, chapter one, verse eight. In the book of Job, chapter one, verse eight. Those who claim direct descendants of the Hebrew Israelites, like the BHI and other groups, teach that they are God's people and everyone else is insignificant, as if no one can be God's people outside of the Hebrew Israelites. They will say that others have the privilege, but the Hebrew Israelites are the teachers of the Word of God.

## Are The Edomites The White Nations

One of the emphases that extremists in the BHI movement express is their disdain for the Edomite. What they mean by this is that the Edomite is equated to the white people, and in the Bible, there were many conflicts between Edom and Israel. This is their way of expressing their mistrust of white people in modern times because they feel that the conflict has always been there, and that is why white people mistreat and oppress black people because blacks are the original Hebrews. This is clearly another fallacy because the scripture does not specify the Edomites' color. I will begin this section with the following scripture:

Genesis 25:19,20,23-26 19 And these are the generations of Isaac, Abraham's son: Abraham begat Isaac: 20, And Isaac was forty years old when he took Rebekah to wife, the daughter of Bethuel the Syrian of Padanaram, the sister to Laban the Syrian. 23 And the Lord said unto her, Two nations are in thy womb, and two manner of people shall be separated from thy bowels; and the one people shall be stronger than the other people; and the elder shall serve the younger. 24 And when her days to be delivered were fulfilled, behold, there were twins in her womb. 25 And the first came out red, all over like a hairy garment; and they called his name Esau. 26 And after that came his brother out, and his hand took hold on Esau's heel; and his name was called Jacob: and Isaac was threescore years old when she bare them.

*Genesis 36:8-9 Thus dwelt Esau in mount Seir: Esau is Edom. 9 And these are the generations of Esau the father of the Edomites in mount Seir:*

*1 Kings 11:14-17 And the Lord stirred up an adversary unto Solomon, Hadad the Edomite: he was of the king's seed in Edom. 15 For it came to pass, when David was in Edom, and Joab the captain of the host was gone up to bury the slain, after he had smitten every male in Edom; 16 (For six months did Joab remain there with all Israel, until he had cut off every male in Edom:) 17 That Hadad fled, he and certain Edomites of his father's servants with him, to go into Egypt; Hadad being yet a little child.*

After reading 1 Kings 11:14-17, we see that Hadad flees to Egypt. At the same time, he was only a child just as the Bible describes JESUS flee into Egypt as a child in Matthew 2:13-15, stating, "And when they were departed, behold, the angel of the Lord appeareth to Joseph in a dream, saying, Arise, and take the young child and his mother, and flee into Egypt, and be thou there until I bring thee word: for Herod will seek the young child to destroy him.

When he arose, he took the young child and his mother by night, and departed into Egypt: And was there until the death of Herod: that it might be fulfilled which was spoken of the Lord by the prophet, saying, Out of Egypt have I called my son (KJV)."

The self-proclaimed BHI would say that JESUS could only hide in Egypt because he was Black. If this statement is true, then the same statement could be true for the Edomite Hadad. In fact, Hadad would have a stronger claim to being of color than JESUS, because when JESUS arrived in Egypt, it was already under the Greek kingdom of Macedon, ruled by Alexander the Great, more than 300 years earlier.

The decision between the self-proclaimed BHI and the white race is built upon a lack of understanding of the lineage of the Israelites and the common ancestor they share with other nations such as the Edomites and other nations even though they do not share the same common ancestor with other nations of color unless we trace everyone common ancestor to Noah which means the entire human race are the same people but GOD divided people at the tower babel where people began to speak different languages and that was the beginning of tribalism.

**Biblical Context**

From a Biblical context: Abraham's covenant with God (Genesis 12:1-3) established him as the father of nations. His descendants would inherit the Promised Land, with Isaac as the covenantal heir. The prophecies concerning Ishmael (Genesis 16:12) foretold that his descendants would be a "wild donkey of a man," dwelling in conflict with others, consistent with the historical Arab tribes. Archaeological evidence from the Levant affirms the existence of Semitic nomads, as described by Abraham. The Edomites and Moabites are frequently mentioned in extrabiblical texts, including the Mesha Stele and Assyrian records, and are often associated with the ancient Israelites.

**Debunking Misinterpretations:**

The BHI's claim that African Americans are the "true Israelites" is inconsistent with genetic evidence, which places ancient Israelites firmly in the Semitic group rather than sub-Saharan Africa. Theological claims about lineage have been co-opted by movements such as the BHI. However, these claims are contradicted by both genetic evidence and Biblical texts, which affirm the ethnic diversity of Abraham's descendants. The BHI movement often misinterprets genealogical and Biblical contexts to claim exclusive Israelite ancestry. African American ancestry is traced to diverse West African origins, not to the Semitic Levant. The misreading of prophecies is a reason for their unification (e.g., Ezekiel 37), which is spiritual and inclusive of all believers rather than physical tribal claims.

# Chapter 6: The Gospel versus Law-Based Ethnic Salvation

**Jesus, Torah, and the New Covenant**

Some BHI sects argue that faith in Christ is insufficient unless one keeps Torah and identifies as Israel. However, Paul teaches that justification is not by "works of the law" but by faith in Christ (Gal. 2:16). Seeking righteousness through the law is to place oneself under a covenant that demands comprehensive obedience (Gal. 3:10).

The law is holy and good, but it cannot give life (Gal. 3:21–22). It exposes sin and points to Christ. In the new covenant, believers fulfill the law's righteous requirement through the Spirit (Rom. 8:1–4), not through ethnic boundary markers.

**Misreading Matthew 5:17**

BHI teachers often quote Jesus as saying, "I have not come to abolish [the Law] but to fulfill," as if "fulfill" means "reinstate Mosaic law unchanged for the church." In Matthew, fulfillment denotes the realization of God's promises and patterns in the Messiah. Jesus fulfills the sacrificial system, priesthood, and temple, which is why the New Testament does not require Gentile believers to become Jews (Acts 15). Jesus did not reinstate the law; the law had to be fulfilled as the prophetic revelation of the suffering Messiah in Isaiah 53 and of the LORD's anointed in Isaiah 61. This is why it was written that Jesus is the one coming in the volume of the book: it was written of him (Ps. 40:7; Heb. 10:7). He abolished the law (Eph. 2:15) and then made a new covenant (Heb. 12:24).

*Ephesians 2:15-17 by abolishing the law of commandments expressed in ordinances, that he might create in himself one new man in place of the two, so making peace, 16 and might reconcile us both to God in one body through the cross, thereby killing the hostility.*

*Colossians 2:14 by canceling the record of debt that stood against us with its legal demands. This he set aside, nailing it to the cross.*

## The Color of Jesus Debate

As noted in the introduction, the self-proclaimed BHI has painted everything in black and white, failing to recognize that it is not entirely black-and-white. Another one of their central doctrines and tools to recruit blacks is the doctrine that Jesus is black. I remember being in Indianapolis, IN, when a few of them approached me. The first thing they showed me was a black photo of Jesus, and they tried to convince me of Jesus' skin color. This approach proves that they are pushing for black supremacy instead of Bible salvation. There have been several radical black movements in the United States over the last two centuries. The first was Garveyism, next the Nation of Islam, then the Black Panther movement, and now the BHI. These movements have been born out of the rejection of white supremacy. White supremacy whitewashes everything, and the BHI is doing the opposite by black washing everything. When black people grow up seeing the image of Christ as a European with long blond hair and blue eyes, it becomes an image that supports the superiority of one race over the other, and the sentiments of this image have been controversial for many years. I can understand the radical mentality of people who stem from these groups. However, the fight against their identity crisis has caused an adverse reaction of delusional thinking.

To deal with this issue of the color of JESUS, let us start here:

John 4:24 God is a Spirit: and they that worship him must worship him in spirit and in truth. KJV

First and foremost, since JESUS is God, we must understand that "God is a spirit" (John 14:6) and that spirits do not have color, race, or ethnicity. The flesh that JESUS came in was for a purpose to fulfill the plan of God, as Paul stated, "Concerning his Son Jesus Christ our Lord, who was made of the seed of David according to the flesh (Romans 1:3)." The flesh was only a vessel to carry the spirit of the LORD on earth to fulfill the messianic ministry of our LORD. The flesh was a "tabernacle" as mentioned in Revelation 21:3. This is why the scripture teaches that: "Jesus Christ has come in the flesh," (1 John 4:3) "came in the likeness of men,"(Philippians 2:7) was in the "likeness of sinful flesh,"(Romans 8:3) and he was "the Word became flesh."(John 1:14) The flesh was not who the Messiah was; it was what he was in, and it had to identify with the people with whom he was in covenant to fulfill prophecy.

Also, it is ridiculous to preach something other than what JESUS commissioned us to preach. The instructions of the LORD were never to preach or teach the color of his skin at any point in his messianic ministry, nor does the Bible make mention of this. This doctrine has no place among people who claim to be representatives of the LORD and ambassadors of the Kingdom of Heaven. If the LORD wanted to promote the color of his skin, then this would constrain the LORD to be only the God of the people who can identify with HIS skin color. The color of the LORD's skin has as much to do with the Bible and salvation as how tall HE was or what size shoes HE wore. This is utterly ridiculous, even to claim the color of HIS skin when John stated, "God is a Spirit: and they that worship him must worship him in spirit and in truth" (John 14:6). Paul made a statement that "for as many as are led by the Spirit of God, they are the sons of God" (Romans 8:14). Not as many as led by the color of God, but his spirit is the emphasis.

I do understand why this is important to the self-proclaimed BHI. They believe that promoting the color of the LORD's skin to be black will liberate the African American person, and it would inspire a more liberated mindset in the black person. This, however, is another fallacy because it is not the promotion of the skin color of the LORD that liberates a person; it is the LORD's spirit. As Paul eloquently exclaims that, "Now the Lord is that Spirit: and where the Spirit of the Lord is, there is liberty" (2 Corinthians 3:17). The reason why we focus on the LORD's spirit and not his skin color is because HE made a promise that he revealed to the prophet Joel that "I will pour out my spirit upon all flesh; and your sons and your daughters shall prophesy, your old men shall dream dreams, your young men shall see visions" (Joel 2:28).  HE did not say I will pour out my spirit upon Jewish flesh, Hebrew flesh, Israelite flesh, but ALL FLESH!

*Out of Egypt I Called My Son*

*Hosea 11:1 When Israel was a child, I loved him, and out of Egypt I called my son (KJV).*

*Matthew 2:15 This was to fulfill what the Lord had spoken by the prophet, 'Out of Egypt I called my son (KJV).*

Some will say, if Jesus is not black, how was he able to hide in Egypt? If a white family with a white child hid in Egypt, they would have been found out with ease. This is an outrageous claim and a far reach because although Egypt is in Africa, there are 53 countries in Africa. From that time until now, everybody in the 53 countries on the continent of Africa is not all the same people and does not look identical to the West Africans that the blacks in America resemble and descend from. When Jesus fled to Egypt, it was the Egypt Alexander the Great conquered in 332 B.C. that had changed the landscape and population. During the 300 years preceding JESUS, Egypt was not the original Egypt; it resembled modern Egypt, with a mixture of people of light and dark complexions.[76]

---

[76] Bosworth, Albert Brian. Conquest and empire: the reign of Alexander the Great. Cambridge University Press, 1993.

# EGYPTIANS 1ST CENTURY BC

Mummy portrait of a young woman, Antinoopolis, Middle Egypt, 2nd century, Louvre, Paris.

Jesus fled to Egypt, and the assumption is that he blended in so well because he had to have been a black man, but this is not a fact because not all people of color call themselves black, as African Americans do. African Americans began identifying as black after going through several preferences of the consensus of what they would like to be called, and black is more of an American construct. It does not represent every person of color in the world.  The majority of humanity is considered people of color. However, people of color do not mean that they are black people who look identical to the black people of West Africa and the United States of America. We will discuss this further in the next chapter on genealogies and haplogroups.

## The Color of the Hebrew

The first falsehood we will examine is the claim that the Bible clearly calls the original Hebrew Israelites black. I first wish to note that I do not subscribe to the notion that the original Hebrews were predominantly white. However, I also do not subscribe to black-washing everything as white supremacists attempt to white-wash everything. The original Hebrews may have been of color, but as this book will clearly explain in the chapter on genealogy and haplogroups, not all people of color belong to the same haplogroup, nation, or tribe. This is validated by the fact that the white population does not even make up one-third of the world's population. Specifically, estimates indicate that white individuals constitute approximately 16% of the global population.[77] This figure is derived from various demographic studies and census data, which indicate that the majority of the world's population resides in regions with significant non-white populations, such as Asia and Africa. For example, the Asian continent alone is home to over 4.5 billion people, while Africa has approximately 1.3 billion residents; both regions are predominantly non-white.[78]

According to the Bible, Noah had three sons, and all three began to populate the world, becoming nations within nations. This gave birth to many people who were considered to be of color that were not Hebrew

---

[77] Painter, Nell Irvin. The history of white people. WW Norton & Company, 2011.

[78] Ellinghaus, Katherine. "Absorbing the 'Aboriginal problem': controlling interracial marriage in Australia in the late 19th and early 20th centuries." Aboriginal History 27 (2003): 183-207.

Israelites because these nations made up the known world at the time, many years before Israel became a nation, so how could a group of radicals stake claim that they are the original Hebrew Israelites from the Bible when numerous nations could be considered to be of color?

According to the United Nations, the global population was estimated at approximately 7.9 billion in 2021. If we consider the populations of Asia, Africa, Latin America, and parts of the Middle East, it is plausible that a substantial majority of these populations could be classified as people of color.[79]

For instance, the Asian continent alone, which includes countries such as China, India, and Indonesia, is home to more than 4.5 billion people, representing more than half of the world's population. Additionally, Africa, with its diverse ethnic groups, accounts for an additional 1.3 billion individuals. Latin America, which includes indigenous, Afro-descendant, and mestizo populations, adds to this demographic mix. Collectively, these regions account for a substantial share of the global population, suggesting that the claim warrants consideration, depending on how "people of color" and "white" populations are defined. How do we know which groups are truly represented as the Hebrew nation? This question cannot just be answered by saying that if you are black, you are the true Hebrews, although the self-proclaimed Hebrew Israelites make this claim through misinterpretations of the Bible.

The primary scripture that has been used is Jeremiah 14:2, where it states, "Judah mourneth, and the gates thereof languish; they are black unto the ground; and the cry of Jerusalem is gone up (KJV)." Scripture manipulation to make the Hebrew black in this scripture does not mean skin color, but is from the Hebrew word קָדַר qâdar, kaw-dar'. The Strong's

---

[79] Arsenovic, Daniela. "Population of the World." (2024): 23-46.

concordance (H6937) shows that this word was translated six times as mourn, four times as black, four times as blackish, once as darkened, and once as heavily. קָדַר qâdar, kaw-dar'; is a primitive root; to be ashy, i.e., dark-colored; by implication, to mourn (in sackcloth or sordid garments): be black(-ish), be (make) dark(-en), × heavily, (cause to) mourn. This scripture describes the emotional or physical despair a person experiences and is unrelated to the person's actual color. The phrase "black unto the ground" is to be understood as "they lie on the ground expressing their sorrow" (NET). The same as the scripture, Jeremiah 8:21 "For the hurt of the daughter of my people am I hurt; I am black; astonishment hath taken hold on me (KJV)." Black in Jeremiah 8:21 is the same Hebrew word, and the latter phrase "I am black; astonishment hath taken hold on me" is translated in the NET "as I go about crying and grieving. I am overwhelmed with dismay," and the note states, "to explain this translation tn Heb "I go about in black [i.e., mourning clothes]. Dismay has seized me." Also, they would use Lamentations 5:10 Our skin was black like an oven because of the terrible famine" (KJV). However, once again, it is a misinterpretation because the Hebrew word for black in this text is כָּמַר kâmar, kaw-mar, which is a primitive root; properly, to intertwine or contract, i.e., (by implication) to shrivel (as with heat); figuratively, to be deeply affected with passion (love or pity): be black, be kindled, yearn. The Strong's concordance (H6937) defines this word as to yearn, be kindled, be black (hot), grow warm and tender, be or grow hot, become hot, become emotionally agitated." This is why, in the NET version, the translation of Lam. 5:10 states, "Our skin is as hot as an oven due to a fever from hunger." The Hebrew word for the color black is שָׁחֹר šāḥōr, shaw-khore', and an example of the scripture that uses this Hebrew word is Zechariah 6:6, where it states, "The black horses which are therein go forth into the north country; and the white go forth after them; and the grisled go forth toward the south country" (KJV). All translations consistently render this Hebrew word as the color black, unlike other Hebrew words that describe a person's emotional and physical condition.

**Examples of Other Nationalities Claiming the Color of Black in the Bible**

The Shulamite woman was a black woman of non-Israelite lineage. However, she professed in **Song of Solomon 1:5-6 I am dark but lovely, O maidens of Jerusalem, dark like the tents of Qedar, lovely like the tent curtains of Salmah. 6 Do not stare at me because I am dark, for the sun has burned my skin. My brothers were angry with me; they made me the keeper of the vineyards. Alas, my own vineyard I could not keep (NET)!** In other words, she was saying not to judge me because I am black, as I have been burned, but I am black and beautiful. The King James Version uses the word black instead of dark, but the word black in this text is the Hebrew word (shaw-khore' - שָׁחֹר) (Strong's Concordance H7838). This is not the same as the manipulation of the self-proclaimed BHI that will use the Hebrew word קָדַר qâdar, kaw-dar', defined by the Strong's concordance (H6937) that shows how this word was translated six times as mourn, four times as black, four times as blackish, one time as darkened, and one time as heavily as mentioned earlier. It is evident that the word used by the BHI to describe blackness is incorrect because the Hebrew word kaw-dar' means to mourn and is not descriptive of the color of skin.

In conclusion, there is not enough evidence to suggest that any one race or ethnicity can claim to be the original Hebrew Israelites if it assumes that they are people of color, because the majority of the known world can be considered people of color. The word black cannot be a blanket term that describes any and everybody who is of color because there were people in African nations who had similar features to African Americans before the Israelite nation was established.

# Chapter 7: Race, Salvation, and the One New Humanity

## Ethnocentrism as a Counterfeit Gospel

A recurring feature of extremist BHI teaching is the claim that God's love and salvation are reserved for one modern ethnic group, while other groups are created for destruction. This is not a biblical election; it is racial determinism. Scripture teaches that God judges individuals and nations for sin, and he calls all people everywhere to repent (Acts 17:30–31).

The Old Testament itself anticipates a multi-ethnic people of God: Israel is chosen so that "all the families of the earth" may be blessed (Gen. 12:3). The prophets foresee nations streaming to the Lord (Isa. 2:2–4). The New Testament announces that vision as reality in Christ (Eph. 3:6).

## What the Bible Means by "Jew," "Israel," and "Gentile" in the New Testament

In the first century, "Jew" typically refers to Judeans and to those affiliated with Jewish identity through lineage and practice. "Gentile" (ethnē) refers to the nations. Paul can speak of a "Jew inwardly" (Rom. 2:28–29), not to erase Jewishness but to emphasize heart-covenant reality, circumcision of the heart by the Spirit. Even before the death of Rehoboam, God looked upon all Israel as a unity, seeing "all Israel in Judah and Benjamin" (2 Chron. 11:3). After the Babylonian captivity, the terms Jew and Israelite are used interchangeably: Ezra calls the returning remnant "Jews" 8 times, "Israel" 40 times. Ezra speaks of "all Israel" (Ezra 2:70; 3:11; 8:35; 10:25 et al.). Nehemiah calls them Jews 11 times and Israel 22 times. Nehemiah speaks of "all Israel being back in the land (Neh 12:47). The remnant who returned from Babylon is represented as "the nation" Mal 1:1).

The second falsehood that the self-proclaimed Black Hebrew Israelites claim is that the word Gentile comes to us in the Bible as a description of the white nations, just as the term Edomite, which we will discuss later in this chapter. To understand the word "Gentile," we must examine it from an etymological perspective. From the beginning of the nation of Israel, the ALMIGHTY GOD was emphasizing the separation of the nation of Israel that worships the one true GOD and the other nations that were paganistic and heathenistic. We will first search the Hebrew usage of the nation from the first time it was used Biblically:

*Gen 12:1-2 Now the LORD had said unto Abram, Get thee out of thy country, and from thy kindred, and from thy father's house, unto a land that I will shew thee: And I will make of thee a great nation, and I will bless thee, and make thy name great; and thou shalt be a blessing.*

The Hebrew word, based on the Strong's concordance, is גוֹי gôwy, go'-ee; rarely (shortened) גֹי gôy; apparently from the same root as H1465 (in the sense of massing); a foreign nation; hence, a Gentile; also (figuratively) a troop of animals, or a flight of locusts: Gentile, heathen, nation, people. "Gentile, a person who is not Jewish. The word stems from the Hebrew term goy, meaning "nation," and was applied to both the Hebrews and other nations. The same Hebrew word is translated as "Gentile" in every instance of its use. Gentile was used only 30 times in the King James Version in the Old Testament, and every time the Hebrew word "goy" denoted a nation, foreign nation, heathen, people, or Gentile. This distinguishing of nations was to sanctify or separate the people of GOD from other nations. GOD did not want the practices of other pagan gods to be adopted into the nation that he chose to be set apart as a holy nation that represented the one true GOD.

Now, when we come to the Greek meaning of Gentile, I would like to begin by using Mark 7:26, which states, "The woman was a Greek, a Syrophenician by nation; and she besought him that he would cast forth the devil out of her daughter (KJV). In this scripture, the word for Greek is Ἑλληνίς Heckēnís, hel-lay-nis'; but the word for nation is γένος génos, ghen'-os, which we get the English word for genetics or genome and gene. The Black Hebrew Israelite will mistakenly use this rendering of Gentile as proof that the Gentiles come from Greek nation which it could be possible because Gentile from the Greek word (Ἑλληνίς Heckēnís, hel-lay-nis'); according to the Strong's concordance has two possible meanings (1) a Greek either by nationality, whether a native of the main land or of the Greek islands or colonies or (2) in the broader sense the name embraces all nations not Jews that made the language, customs, and learning of the Greeks their own; the primary reference is to a difference of religion and worship. There are only 27 instances in the Bible where the Greek word for "Gentile," Ἕλλην (heckēn), is used. Both definitions are correct because the Jews were living under Roman-Greek rule and at times would discuss the difference between the Jew and the Greek. However, the second definition that makes a difference between the Jew and other nations is the most common way to use the term "Gentile."

The most common usage of the word "Gentile" comes from the Koine Greek word ἔθνος éthnos, eth'-nos; from Strong's concordance (G1484), which means a race (as of the same habit), i.e., a tribe; especially, a foreign (non-Jewish) one (usually, by implication, pagan): Gentile, heathen, nation, people. This word occurs 152 times in the Biblical scriptures; over sixty times it is translated as "Gentile," and over eighty times as "nation." This pertains more to the Hebrew term for "Gentile" or "nation". Gentile can be used for any nation, especially a nation that is non-Jewish, but it speaks to the difference in ethnicity among people. We will further go into more depth about Gentile in chapter 9.

## Is Salvation Only To The Jews?

*Romans 3:29 Is he the God of the Jews only? Is he not also of the Gentiles? Yes, of the Gentiles also: (KJV)*

Another fallacy by the self-proclaimed BHI is that the LORD only came for the Jews, and salvation is only a right of the Jews. I note that self-proclaimed BHI doctrines may differ in their beliefs regarding some of these aspects, but many I have encountered consistently hold this view. The question is, how can the LORD come only for the Jews? It is true in a sense that the LORD came to the Jews initially because John 1:11 states, "He came unto his own, and his own received him not (KJV). In other words, he came to the Jews, and they rejected him. This was something that was supposed to happen according to Biblical prophecy in the book of Isaiah, chapter 53, verses 3 and 4 state, "He is despised and rejected of men; a man of sorrows, and acquainted with grief: and we hid as it were our faces from him; he was despised, and we esteemed him not.  Surely he hath borne our griefs, and carried our sorrows: yet we did esteem him stricken, smitten of God, and afflicted (KJV)."  This was a sign that identified the Messiah. He would perform great miracles and healings among his people, and they would reject him despite his fulfillment of the prophecies about what the Messiah would do when he came. The results of the rejection are that the Jews as a nation rejected JESUS as the Messiah. Another example in the scripture is John chapter 12, where it states, **"37 But though he had done so many miracles before them, yet they believed not on him: 38 That the saying of Esaias the prophet might be fulfilled, which he spake, Lord, who hath believed our report? and to whom hath the arm of the**

**Lord been revealed (KJV)?"** This is why he did no more miracles in Nazareth, due to their unbelief, according to Matthew 13:58 and Mark 6:5.

**How can salvation only be for the Jews?**

*John 3:16 For God so loved the world, that he gave his only begotten Son, that whosoever believeth in him should not perish, but have everlasting life. (KJV)*

Notice the scripture does not say For God so loved the Jew or Hebrew, but it states that HE loves the world and whosoever believeth, not whosoever believes that is a Jew or Hebrew. I will go even further to state that the LORD's final instructions to his disciples in Luke 14:27 state, "And that repentance and remission of sins should be preached in his name among all nations, beginning at Jerusalem" (KJV). Likewise, in Matthew 28:19, it states, "Go ye therefore, and teach all nations, baptizing them in the name of the Father, and of the Son, and of the Holy Ghost: (KJV)." Also, in Mark 16:15, it states, "And he said unto them, Go ye into all the world, and preach the gospel to every creature (KJV)." The LORD wanted the disciples to go into the world and preach the gospel, namely, the good news that salvation belongs to everyone, not just the Jews or the Hebrews. HE did not say go and preach or teach them to the Jew but to "every creature", "all nations," and people groups. To say that the LORD only came to save the Jew/Hebrew is a gross neglect of scripture and a total manipulation of people's minds. This is the fallacy that the self-proclaimed BHI practice when they read into the scripture their own personal interpretation, which is considered eisegesis; a misinterpretation of scripture where someone reads into a text their personal assumption or bias, the opposite of exegesis.

Another point that I will like to point out concerning the fallacy of the self-proclaimed BHI when it comes to salvation only to the Jews and that is found in the book of **Revelation 7:9**. It states, **"After this I beheld, and, lo, a great multitude, which no man could number, of all nations, and kindreds, and people, and tongues, stood before the throne, and before the Lamb, clothed with white robes, and palms in their hands" (KJV).** Many BHI believe that all nations, kindreds, people, and tongues are only speaking of Jewish people, ignoring the fact that the word nations is the Greek word ethnos, meaning ethnicities, nations, and is translated in other parts of the Bible as Gentiles. Also, the previous verses describe 144,000 Jewish people chosen by the LORD to be sealed. Revelation 7:9 shows how there will be every nation, tribe, people, and language, standing before the throne and it is distinct from the list of the twelve thousand from each tribe of Israel mentioned before the this text in verses 4-8  which is appropriate due to it follows the pattern of the Biblical prophecy in the book of Zechariah 8:23 where it states, "Thus saith the Lord of hosts; In those days it shall come to pass, that ten men shall take hold out of all languages of the nations, even shall take hold of the skirt of him that is a Jew, saying, We will go with you: for we have heard that God is with you (KJV)." In the days of tribulation there will other nations that will hear the message of the Jewish nation and will follow them because as the scripture teaches, "these are they that came out of great tribulation" (Romans 7:14), and the Jew is the ones who will be preaching about the LORD in the days of the tribulation because right now they are blinded according to **Romans 11:25, that states, "For I would not, brethren, that ye should be ignorant of this mystery, lest ye should be wise in your own conceits; that blindness in part is happened to Israel, until the fulness of the Gentiles be come in."** In other words, the Jewish nation's hearts were hardened and could not receive JESUS as the Messiah as a nation. The prophecies of Zechariah, chapter eight, and Revelation, chapter seven, would not come to pass until the full number of Gentiles comes into the kingdom of GOD.

It must be noted that there were some Jews who received JESUS and followed his teachings when he was revealed on earth. Many followed him and accepted Jesus as the Messiah because HE used them extensively in the inception of the church, but as a nation, they rejected him. As a nation, they are blind, even though there are individuals who are Jewish/Hebrew or of Israelite genealogy that will be saved, but the nations as a whole are blind. So, in this regard, if the self-proclaimed BHI are the true Jews, then why would anyone listen to them, because according to Romans 11:25, they are blind and their hearts are hardened. However, they are not the true Hebrews of the Bible but they are still blind and do not know what they are talking about because they are spreading a latter-day doctrine or teaching that is considered a doctrine of devils that will be revealed in the latter times according to 1 Timothy chapter 4 verse 1: *"Now the Spirit speaketh expressly, that in the latter times some shall depart from the faith, giving heed to seducing spirits, and doctrines of devils (KJV)."*

Let us explore this claim that the LORD came only to save the Jew/Hebrew.

*Galatians 3:28,29 There is neither Jew nor Greek, there is neither bond nor free, there is neither male nor female: for ye are all one in Christ Jesus. And if ye be Christ's, then are ye Abraham's seed, and heirs according to the promise (KJV).*

We must realize that the Bible does not hold a claim that supports the teachings of the self-proclaimed BHI because Paul declares that to be in Christ is not predicated on a person's race or ethnicity, their status quo, or gender. Paul also states, **"For I am not ashamed of the gospel of Christ:**

**for it is the power of God unto salvation to everyone that believeth; to the Jew first, and also to the Greek" (Romans 1:16).** Why would Paul make these claims? Was Paul disobedient to the LORD, or was he on a mission for the LORD, and he knew **"that I should preach among the Gentiles the unsearchable riches of Christ" (Ephesians 3:8)?** During Paul's missionary journeys, he preached to a majority of non-Jews and even got into a major rift with Peter over the way he treated the Gentile believers. Was the house of Cornelius a Jewish home? Was Cornelius Hebrew by nature? Absolutely not! However, it did not stop the LORD's disciples from going to his house, and the LORD wrought salvation for the Gentile house of Cornelius. Peter even stated, "Of a truth I perceive that God is no respecter of persons" (Acts 10:34). There are many other scriptures that could be used to make it clear that salvation is for all people, regardless of their racial identity. The most common usage of the word "Gentile" comes from the Koine Greek word ἔθνος éthnos, eth'-nos; from Strong's concordance (G1484). Gentiles are defined as ethnicities, which is an umbrella term in the Bible for all nations other than Jews.

*Grafted in:*

*Romans 9:25 As he saith also in Osee, I will call them my people, which were not my people; and her beloved, which was not beloved. KJV*

*Romans 11:17 And if some of the branches be broken off, and thou, being a wild olive tree, wert grafted in among them, and with them partakest of the root and fatness of the olive tree; KJV*

The Bible is clear on this subject that the Gentiles or nonbelievers were called the people of God when the covenanted people rebelled against the LORD. For that reason, the LORD grafted the Gentiles into the family to be heirs of Abraham. Let us look at the rest of Paul's dissertation in *Romans 11:*

*11 I say then, Have they stumbled that they should fall? God forbid: but rather through their fall salvation is come unto the Gentiles, for to provoke them to jealousy.*

*12 Now if the fall of them be the riches of the world, and the diminishing of them the riches of the Gentiles; how much more their fulness?*

*13 For I speak to you Gentiles, inasmuch as I am the apostle of the Gentiles, I magnify mine office:*

*14 If by any means I may provoke to emulation them which are my flesh, and might save some of them.*

*15 For if the casting away of them be the reconciling of the world, what shall the receiving of them be, but life from the dead?*

I have underlined some points in this text to show the condition of the Jews and the Gentiles as it relates to salvation. First of all, Israel is in a fallen condition that produced salvation for non-Jews. Secondly, Paul was a Jew according to the flesh but was commissioned to preach to the Gentiles (non-Jews). Thirdly, Paul hoped some of them would be saved because, as a nation, they are blinded until the fullness of the Gentiles comes in (Romans 11:25). Paul had a burden for his people, even though his mission was to evangelize the non-Jewish world. This is why he petitioned God at the beginning of Romans 10:1, stating, "Brothers and sisters, my heart's desire and prayer to God on behalf of my fellow Israelites is for their salvation."

The Bible is clearly against the teachings of the self-proclaimed BHI; Paul, Peter, and the apostles don't support them; and most definitely, the LORD does not support their claims. The holy scriptures are clear on this subject. The LORD always intended to include all people into his fold and come to the knowledge of the LORD, for the LORD stated through his prophet Isaiah that, "It is a light thing that thou shouldest be my servant to raise up the tribes of Jacob, and to restore the preserved of Israel: I will also give thee for a light to the Gentiles, that thou mayest be my salvation unto the end of the earth (Isaiah 46:9, KJV)." This Old Testament scripture shows that God always intended to evangelize all nations of the world.

*Another definitive text is Joel 2:28*

*And it shall come to pass afterward, that I will pour out my spirit upon all flesh; and your sons and your daughters shall prophesy, your old men shall dream dreams, your young men shall see visions: (KJV)*

In this text, the LORD clearly states that he planned to pour out His Spirit upon all flesh. Not just Jewish/Hebrew flesh but all flesh, and then proclaimed in verse 32, "that whosoever shall call on the name of the Lord shall be delivered." This prophetic scripture came to pass on the day of Pentecost, as described in the book of Acts: when the LORD's spirit was poured out, it was poured out on both Jews and proselytes, non-Jews who had converted to the worship of the YAHWEH God. They came from all nations for their yearly pilgrimage to Jerusalem.

*Acts 2:8-11,16 And how hear we every man in our own tongue, wherein we were born?*

*9 Parthians, and Medes, and Elamites, and the dwellers in Mesopotamia, and in Judaea, and Cappadocia, in Pontus, and Asia,*

*10 Phrygia, and Pamphylia, in Egypt, and in the parts of Libya about Cyrene, and strangers of Rome, Jews and proselytes,*

*11 Cretes and Arabians, we do hear them speak in our tongues the wonderful works of God.*

*16 But this is that which was spoken by the prophet Joel;*

This is just further proof that salvation is not only for the Jews/Hebrew race but for all people who are willing to acknowledge, worship, and obey the one, true, and living God!

## Biology Does Not Concern GOD

*28 For a person is not a Jew who is one outwardly, nor is circumcision something that is outward in the flesh, 29 but someone is a Jew who is one inwardly, and circumcision is of the heart[ay] by the Spirit and not by the letter. This person's praise is not from people but from God. (NET)*

In chapter two of Romans, Paul argues that God shows no respect for persons. He expresses how being a Jew outwardly, or in other words, biologically, does not make you a Jew, nor does circumcision. In contrast, GOD is more concerned about the circumcision of the heart, which makes you more of a Jew than your biology. The Holy Spirit gives the circumcision of the heart, as it states in verse 29, which allows the adoption of GOD to take place, and that is the circumcision of the heart. Colossians 2:11also says, "In whom also ye are circumcised with the circumcision made without hands, in putting off the body of the sins of the flesh by the circumcision of Christ (KJV)."

I will present another scripture that demonstrates a lack of concern for lineage in the book of **Romans 9:6-8:**

*6 It is not as though the word of God had failed. For not all those who are descended from Israel are truly Israel, 7 nor are all the children of Abraham true descendants; rather, "through Isaac will your descendants be counted." 8 This means it is not the children of the flesh[d] who are the children of God; rather, the children of promise are counted as descendants. (NET)*

It is evident that not all of Israel is considered to be of Israel, just as not all of those who call themselves Christians are considered to be Christians by GOD.

# Chapter 8: Africa, the Bible, and Historical Integrity

## Africans in Scripture without the BHI Mythology

The Bible speaks frequently about Africa and Africans (e.g., Egypt/Mizraim, Cush/Kush). These references are not secret codes for "Israelites." They are straightforward in geography and history: African peoples appear as neighbors, allies, and enemies, and, importantly, as participants in God's saving story (e.g., the Ethiopian eunuch in Acts 8:26–40). There were ancient African kingdoms long before Israel's formation.[80]

Affirming African presence in the Bible does not require claiming that West African peoples are secretly ancient Israelites. It is enough and more accurate to say that God has always been at work among the nations, including in Africa.

One thing we must understand is that Africa is a continent with 53 countries and over 3,000 ethnic groups. With that understanding, the majority of the people groups of Africa have always been over 95% people of color. This is why it is outrageous for BHI members to say that African Americans were the descendants of the true Hebrew Israelites, because there were over 12 million Africans who were in the slave trade, who were from hundreds of different ethnic groups and tribes across West and Central Africa. Also, since there were already developed nations in Africa that predate Israel, then even if there were some Jews that resembled the Africans, how would we know who are the true descendants and who are just indigenous to Africa? This is why the BHI claims are extreme and are impossible to be absolute in describing all African Americans and black people as one group of people that descended from Jacob's lineage.

---

[80] Basil Davidson, The African Past: Chronicles from Antiquity to Modern Times (London: Longman, 1964), 19–34.

## West African Civilizations Predate Israel as a Nation

BHI rhetoric sometimes implies that West Africans did not have a meaningful history before "Israelite" identity. That is historically false. African civilizations and empires developed complex political and economic systems independent of Israel's emergence as a nation. For example, the Ghana Empire (8th–13th centuries CE), Mali (13th–16th centuries), and Songhai (15th–16th centuries) were major West African states tied into trans-Saharan trade and intellectual networks.[81]

This point matters because it frees African history from the false choice between "no history" and "Israelite history." Africa has its own deep and dignified past, and Christian faith does not require rewriting that past into a different people's story.[82]

Cush is mentioned several times in the Book of Jeremiah, both as a geographical location and as a personal name. Although debates persist among scholars over whether Cush, as a geographical location, refers to Africa or Mesopotamia, I think that, throughout the Old Testament, Cush refers nowhere but to Africa and to persons of African ancestry.[83]

In the Major Prophets, the terms used to refer to Africa and Africans appear more than 180 times. Cush also appears as a geographical location. Cushi was also used as a name, as in Jeremiah 36:14, where the ancestors of Yehudi, the prince who read Jeremiah's scroll to King Jehoiakim, were

---

[81] Conrad, David C. *Empires of Medieval West Africa: Ghana, Mali, and Songhay.* Infobase Publishing, 2010.

[82] Mohamed, Hani Abdirachid, 2023. "African Civilization: From Ancient Kingdoms to Modern Societies", *International Journal of Social Science and Human Research*(06), 06. https://doi.org/10.47191/ijsshr/v6-i6-11

[83] Monges, Miriam Ma'at-Ka-Re. *Kush: an Afrocentric Perspective.* 1995. Temple University, PhD dissertation. search.proquest.com, https://search.proquest.com/openview/7fb5fe7e8028831ebbbfde11ceccf52b/1?pq-origsite=gscholar&cbl=18750&diss=y.

traced to Cushi. Ebed-Melech, the Cushite who delivered one of the greatest prophets, Jeremiah, from death, is also mentioned in Jeremiah. He was specifically described as a Cushi. Notably, while "Cush" or "Egypt" occurs 53 times in the LXX, it occurs 67 times in the MT in the book of Jeremiah. This indicates that the prophet Jeremiah is very familiar with Africans (Cush or Egypt).[84]

The history of Africa is rich and complex, featuring numerous great and mighty nations that predate the establishment of the original nation of Israel. These civilizations played significant roles in the development of human culture, trade, and governance long before Israel emerged as a political entity.

One of the most notable ancient civilizations in Africa is Ancient Egypt, often regarded as one of the earliest and most influential in human history. The civilization of Ancient Egypt, with its advanced social structure, monumental architecture, and contributions to writing and mathematics, flourished along the Nile River for thousands of years, beginning around 3100 BCE.[85] Egypt's influence extended beyond its borders, shaping neighboring regions and contributing to the ancient world's cultural and political landscape.

Another significant civilization was the Kingdom of Kush, located south of Egypt in present-day Sudan. The Kingdom of Kush emerged around 1070 BCE and is known for its wealth, military power, and the establishment of a dynasty that ruled Egypt during the 25th Dynasty.[86] The

---

[84] Kurewa, John Wesley Zwomunondiita. African Religion: The quarry of the rock of monotheism. Upper Room Books, 2016.

[85] Setiawati, D., N. K. Ramadani, and S. Lestari. "The Contribution of Ancient Egypt Civilization to Life in the World." Journal of Religion and Social Change, vol. 1, no. 1, 2024, pp. 1-10.

[86] Kahn, Dan'el. "The history of Kush—an outline." The power of walls-Fortifications in ancient northeastern Africa. Proceedings of the Inter national

Kushites were known for their impressive pyramids and their role as a cultural bridge between Sub-Saharan Africa and the Mediterranean world.

The Carthaginian Empire, centered in present-day Tunisia, was another powerful entity that existed from the 9th century BCE until its destruction by Rome in 146 BCE. Carthage was a major trading hub and a formidable maritime power, known for its conflicts with Rome during the Punic Wars.[87] The Carthaginians developed a rich culture that included advancements in agriculture, trade, and military strategy.

In West Africa, the Ghana Empire (circa 300-1200 CE) was among the earliest known empires, flourishing through its control of the trans-Saharan trade routes. The empire was renowned for its wealth, particularly in gold, and its sophisticated governance structures.[88] Following Ghana, the Mali Empire rose to prominence in the 13th century, with its capital, Timbuktu, becoming a center of learning and culture that attracted scholars from across the Islamic world.[89]

The Great Zimbabwe civilization, which thrived from the 11th to the 15th centuries in present-day Zimbabwe, is another example of a powerful African nation. Known for its impressive stone structures and trade networks, Great Zimbabwe was a center of commerce and culture in southeastern Africa.[90] The civilization's decline coincided with the rise of other regional powers, but its legacy remains significant in the study of African history.

---

Workshop held at the University of Cologne, 4th-7th August 2011. Colloquium Africanum. Vol. 5. 2013.

[87] Merdinger, Jane, Jesse A. Hoover, and Nancy Weatherwax. Religion at Carthage 800 BCE-439 CE: From Baal-Hammon to Christ. Vol. 191. Brill, 2025.

[88] Akrong, A. O. "Trade, routes, trade, and commerce in pre-colonial Africa." Springer Gender, Springer, 2019, pp. 65-82.

[89] Conrad, David C. Empires of Medieval West Africa: Ghana, Mali, and Songhay. Infobase Publishing, 2010.

[90] Fontein, Joost, and Neil L. Norman. "The silence of Great Zimbabwe: contested landscapes and the power of heritage." (2009).

Additionally, the Aksumite Empire, located in modern-day Ethiopia and Eritrea, emerged around the 1st century CE and became a major trading empire, known for its monumental obelisks and for being one of the first states to adopt Christianity officially.[91] The Aksumites played a crucial role in trade between Africa, the Middle East, and beyond, establishing a legacy that influenced subsequent civilizations.

In summary, the history of Africa before the establishment of Israel is marked by several major civilizations, including Ancient Egypt, the Kingdom of Kush, the Carthaginian Empire, the Ghana and Mali Empires, Great Zimbabwe, and the Aksumite Empire. Each of these nations contributed to the rich tapestry of human history, showcasing Africa's role as a cradle of civilization.

---

[91] Woldekiros, Helina Solomon. The boundaries of ancient trade: kings, commoners, and the Aksumite salt trade of Ethiopia. University Press of Colorado, 2023.

# Chapter 9: Misinformation: Definitions, Etymologies, and Propaganda

## Common Misinformation Patterns

Modern BHI apologetics often relies on a predictable set of rhetorical moves: (1) redefining words (e.g., "Gentile," "Jew," "Edom"), (2) building arguments from sound-alike words ("niger" = "Negro" = "Niger" = "Nigeria"), (3) quoting sources out of context, and (4) appealing to conspiracy to explain why mainstream historians "hide the truth."

## Word Games Are Not Exegesis

Biblical interpretation requires context, grammar, genre, and historical setting. Claims that an English or Latin word "proves" a biblical identity typically ignore that the Bible was written primarily in Hebrew, Aramaic, and Greek. Similar-sounding words across languages can be a coincidence; they are not evidence of descent.

"The seed of Edom, the seed of Cain, the Synagogue of Satan, and Lucifer himself are the major confederates that have been against us for a very long time."[92]

The term "niger" has been taken out of context by the BHI by equating it the derogatory term of "Nigga," because of its meaning and the term "niger" has been taken out of context by the BHI by equating it the derogatory term of "Nigga," because of its meaning, and will use this as a point of proof that the Jews were black. This is an extreme interpretation of a word used only once in the New Testament to describe a single man, Simeon. The text reads as follows: ***"Now there were in the church that***

---

[92] Center on Extremism, "Hebrews to Negroes: What You Need to Know," ADL, last modified November 11, 2022,

*was at Antioch certain prophets and teachers; as Barnabas, and Simeon that was called Niger, and Lucius of Cyrene, and Manaen, which had been brought up with Herod the tetrarch, and Saul" (Acts 13:1).* If this were a derogatory term to display disdain towards the Jews then the word would have been used more frequently. The word "niger" was used to distinguish Simeon from Barnabas and Lucius. Lucius distinguished himself by stating that he was from Cyrene, and Barnabas was a Levite from Cyprus, according to Acts 4:36. It can be inferred that Simeon was unlike his other two companions; the text described him as black. Another point to note was the diversity of the group mentioned in Acts 13:1. Barnabas was a Levite; Simeon was a black man, likely from Africa; Lucius was a Cyrenean from Northern Libya; Manaen was a nobleman with ties to Herod's family; and Saul was a Jewish Pharisee. This example of the early church's diversity further strengthens the argument that salvation is for everyone, regardless of race, ethnicity, or lineage.

## "Gentile" (Hebrew goy; Greek ethnos)

In Scripture, "Gentile" means "nations", peoples outside Israel's covenant community. It does not mean "white," "European," or "enemy." In fact, Israel itself can be called a "nation" (goy) in covenant language (Exod. 19:6).

The Hebrew word based on the Strong's concordance is גּוֹי gôwy, go'-ee; rarely (shortened) גֹּי gôy; apparently from the same root as H1465 (in the sense of massing); a foreign nation; hence, a Gentile; also (figuratively) a troop of animals, or a flight of locusts:—Gentile, heathen, nation, people. "Gentile, a person who is not Jewish. The word stems from the Hebrew term goy, which means "nation," and was applied both to the Hebrews and to other nations. The plural, goyim, especially with the definite article ha-goyim, "the nations," referred to the nations of the world that were not

Hebrew.[93] This same Hebrew word is also translated as "Gentile" every time it is used. "Gentile" was used only 30 times in the King James Version of the Old Testament, and every time the Hebrew word was "goy," which stood for nation, foreign nation, heathen, people, and Gentile. This distinguishing of nations was to sanctify or separate the people of GOD from other nations. GOD did not want the practices of other pagan gods to be adopted into the nation that he chose to be set apart as a holy nation that represented the one true GOD.

Now, when we come to the Greek meaning of Gentile, I would like to begin by using Mark 7:26, which states, "The woman was a Greek, a Syrophenician by nation; and she besought him that he would cast forth the devil out of her daughter (KJV). In this scripture, the word for Greek is Ἑλληνίς Heckēnís, hel-lay-nis'; but the word for nation is γένος génos, ghen'-os, which we get the English word for genetics or genome and gene. The Black Hebrew Israelite will mistakenly use this rendering of Gentile as proof that the Gentiles come from Greek nation which it could be possible because Gentile from the Greek word (Ἑλληνίς Heckēnís, hel-lay-nis'); according to the Strong's concordance has two possible meanings (1) a Greek either by nationality, whether a native of the main land or of the Greek islands or colonies or (2) in a wider sense the name embraces all nations not Jews that made the language, customs, and learning of the Greeks their own; the primary reference is to a difference of religion and worship. There are only 27 times in the Bile where the Greek word for "Gentile" comes from Ἕλλην (heckēn) is used. Both definitions are correct because the Jews were living under Roman-Greek rule and at times would discuss the difference between the Jew and the Greek. However, the second

---

[93] "Gentile," Encyclopedia Britannica, last modified July 20, 1998, https://www.britannica.com/topic/Gentile.

definition that makes a difference between the Jew and other nations is the most common way to use the term "Gentile."

The most common usage of the word "Gentile" comes from the Koine Greek word ἔθνος éthnos, eth'-nos; from Strong's concordance (G1484), which means a race (as of the same habit), i.e., a tribe; especially, a foreign (non-Jewish) one (usually, by implication, pagan): Gentile, heathen, nation, people. This word is used 152 times in the Biblical scriptures; over 60 times it is translated as Gentile, and over 80 times as nation. This is more specifically related to the Hebrew word for "Gentile" or "nation". Gentile can be used for any nation, especially a nation that is non-Jewish, but it speaks to the difference in ethnicity among people.

If we dive deeper into the etymology of the word "Gentile," we will also see a Latin usage, where the Vulgate translates the Greek ethnikos, from ta ethne "the nations," which translates Hebrew ha goyim "the (non-Jewish) nations.[94]  Hence, in Late Latin, after the Christianization of Rome, gentilis could also mean "pagans, heathens," as opposed to Christians. It extends to "of the same family or clan, from gens (genitive gentis) "race, clan," from PIE root gene- "give birth, beget," with derivatives referring to procreation and familial and tribal groups.[95] So, it is evidently clear that the word "Gentile" is mainly used as a term that distinguishes the Jews from all other nations and has little to do with white nations.

## Misuse of Hitler and Modern Polemics

Some BHI content attempts to validate its racial categories by quoting modern political propaganda, including Nazi material, or by

---

[94] Duling, Dennis C. "Ethnicity, ethnocentrism, and the Matthean ethnos." Biblical Theology Bulletin 35.4 (2005): 125-143.

[95] Gaca, Kathy L., and Laurence L. Welborn, eds. Early patristic readings of Romans. A&C Black, 2005.

misrepresenting what Hitler wrote about race. This is a theological dead end. Christians do not build doctrine on twentieth-century racial ideology; we build it on Scripture interpreted in the communion of the historic church.

The 2018 film Hebrews to Negroes, based on director Ronald Dalton Jr.'s book series of the same name, is a three-plus-hour effort to "prove" the Black Hebrew Israelite (BHI) belief that certain people of color, including Black Americans, are the true descendants of the biblical Israelites. Statement falsely attributed to Adolf Hitler that is shown during the film; an example of the film's use of quotes -- real and falsified -- from prominent antisemites as "evidence" to support its claims.

"The Americans plan on moving these false white Jews into a state of Israel. Because the white Jews know that the Negroes are the real children of Israel, and to keep America's secret, the Jews will blackmail America. They will extort America; their plan for world domination will not work if the Negroes know who they are." This is a fabricated "quotation" falsely attributed to Adolf Hitler.[96]

"America has God's Jewelry, The Americans have the jewels of God. The Americans have stolen God's precious jewels. "What do you mean his precious jewels?" THE SOLDIER ASKED, Hitler said, "America has stolen the Jews. The Jewels of God. His Jewelry. The NEGROES. They are the TRUE HEBREWS. What a foolish move and a direct challenge to God. And they plan on moving these false white Jews into a state of Israel."

"Because the white Jews know that the Negroes are the Real Children of Israel and to keep America's secret the Jews will blackmail America. They will extort America, their plan for world domination won't work if the Negroes know who they are."

Believed to be said by Adolph Hitler in a secret document before his death in an undisclosed location.

Source: Center on Extremism. "Hebrews to Negroes: What You Need to Know." ADL. Last modified November 11, 2022.

---

[96] Center on Extremism, "Hebrews to Negroes: What You Need to Know," ADL, last modified November 11, 2022.

This statement, falsely attributed to Adolf Hitler, is shown during the film; an example of the film's use of quotes -- real and falsified -- from prominent antisemites as "evidence" to support its claims.

Below is from the book "The Nazis." On page 132, it states under the picture of Hitler the following: "In one segment of a Nazi "instructional" film (right), the genetic heritage of the Jew is purportedly traced to Oriental, Negro, Near Asian and Hamitic peoples. Hence, the film concludes, "the Jew is a bastard." The book never claimed that America has the real jewels of God, alluding to African Americans.

Source: Herzstein, Robert E. The Nazis. Time Life Medical, 1980, 132-133.

Below is a historical marker located in Israel Hill, Virginia, which is another attempt by BHI to use as evidence that descendants of enslaved Africans were the Israelites of the Bible. When reading the historical marker, it was clear that Judith and Richard Randolph's unique act of giving land to freed enslaved African Americans was celebrated as a symbolic reference to the Biblical account of the Israelites being freed from bondage and given land of their own. The formerly enslaved people who established the community in 1810-1811 identified with the biblical story of the Israelites' escape from bondage and their settlement in a "Promised Land" of their own.

Photographed by Craig Swain, February 27, 2010

This urban legend surrounding Israel Hill, Virginia, is not to be taken literally as BHI proponents do. The formerly enslaved people who founded the city did not consider themselves descendants of Jacob. They referred to themselves as Israelites in tribute to the land of "Israel," which was granted to them. It is also notable that the church founded there in 1836 was Baptist, not a Jewish Synagogue or a Temple.

# Chapter 10: Israel in Prophecy

This chapter is important because the BHI movement is delusional in its understanding of prophecy. If the BHI members are the true Israelites, along with any other group that believes that, then they will have to have possession of Jerusalem as a nation. Most BHI members do not occupy their own neighborhoods or cities, so how would they occupy the nation of Israel? They definitely could not go over to Israel and demand that the nation be turned over because Israel is one of the most formidable military forces in the world. This chapter will show Israel in the light of prophecy and how whoever occupies Israel during the end times is the people the Bible is referring to as Jews.

From a futurist reading of biblical prophecy, the central stage of end-time events is Jerusalem and the nation of Israel. Scripture makes this plain. Revelation 11:3–8 declares that God will raise up two witnesses who will prophesy in Jerusalem for 1,260 days. The text identifies the city as "the great city... where also our Lord was crucified" (Revelation 11:8), which unmistakably points to Jerusalem. This shows that in the last days, God's prophetic dealings will again focus heavily on Israel and its covenant land.

The Bible also teaches that a coming world ruler, commonly called the Antichrist, will arise with unusual political skill, spiritual deception, and persuasive power. Daniel 9:27 speaks of a ruler who will confirm a covenant with many for one week, and 2 Thessalonians 2:3–4 describes "that man of sin" who will exalt himself above all that is called God and sit in the temple of God, showing himself to be God. Jesus referred to this same event in Matthew 24:15 when He warned, "When ye therefore shall see the abomination of desolation, spoken of by Daniel the prophet, stand in the holy place..." This warning is directly tied to Judea, Jerusalem, and the temple, demonstrating that Matthew 24 must be understood in its prophetic context as describing events that concern Israel in the last days.

At first, this deceptive ruler will appear acceptable to many because he will come in his own name and be received by those who reject the true Messiah, just as Jesus warned in John 5:43: "I am come in my Father's name, and ye receive me not: if another shall come in his own name, him ye will receive." However, his true character will be exposed when he desecrates the temple and sets up the abomination of desolation. At that moment, faithful Jews will recognize that he cannot be the promised Messiah, because idolatry is utterly contrary to the law of God. The commandment is clear: "Thou shalt have no other gods before me. Thou shalt not make unto thee any graven image" (Exodus 20:3–4). Likewise, Deuteronomy 6:4 declares, "Hear, O Israel: The Lord our God is one Lord." The setting up of an idol in the holy place will reveal him not as Israel's deliverer, but as a false Christ and blasphemer.

This is why Matthew 24 is so important. Jesus was not giving a vague, generalized description of suffering for all people in all ages; He was answering Jewish questions about the sign of His coming and the end of the age (Matthew 24:3). His references to "Judaea" (Matthew 24:16), "the sabbath day" (Matthew 24:20), and "the holy place" (Matthew 24:15) all show that this prophecy is deeply rooted in Israel's prophetic future. The passage harmonizes with Daniel 12:1, Jeremiah 30:7, and Zechariah 13:8–9, each of which speaks of an unparalleled time of trouble connected with Jacob, Israel, and the refining of the Jewish people.

Jeremiah 30:7 calls this period "the time of Jacob's trouble," yet it also promises that "he shall be saved out of it." Daniel 12:1 likewise says, "there shall be a time of trouble, such as never was since there was a nation," but adds that "thy people shall be delivered, every one that shall be found written in the book." Zechariah 13:8–9 further reveals that Israel will pass through severe refining, and a remnant will emerge in faith, saying, "The Lord is my God." These passages show that God is not finished with Israel; rather, He will use the tribulation to bring a remnant of the Jewish people to repentance and faith in their true Messiah.

This future national awakening is also taught in Zechariah 12:10: "And I will pour upon the house of David, and upon the inhabitants of Jerusalem, the spirit of grace and of supplications: and they shall look upon me whom they have pierced." The result is mourning, repentance, and spiritual cleansing, which continues into Zechariah 13:1: "In that day there shall be a fountain opened to the house of David and to the inhabitants of Jerusalem for sin and for uncleanness." Paul echoes this same truth in Romans 11:25–27, where he explains that "blindness in part has happened to Israel, until the fulness of the Gentiles be come in. And so all Israel shall be saved." This does not mean every ethnic Jew of all time, but it does point to a future salvation of the repentant remnant of Israel when the Deliverer comes out of Zion.

Zechariah 8:23 also speaks powerfully about Israel's future significance: "Thus saith the Lord of hosts; In those days it shall come to pass, that ten men shall take hold out of all languages of the nations, even shall take hold of the skirt of him that is a Jew, saying, We will go with you: for we have heard that God is with you." In prophetic language, these "ten men" represent the nations of the world. The picture is not merely of individuals admiring a Jew, but of the nations recognizing that God's covenant purposes are being manifested through Israel. This corresponds with other passages that foresee the nations coming to Jerusalem in the kingdom age, such as Isaiah 2:2–4, Micah 4:1–3, and Zechariah 14:16. Isaiah declares that "all nations shall flow unto it," and many people will say, "Come ye, and let us go up to the mountain of the Lord." Thus, Zechariah 8:23 points to a day when the nations will acknowledge that God has uniquely intervened on behalf of His ancient people.

The prophets repeatedly affirm that the Jewish people will be regathered and restored in the last days. Deuteronomy 30:1–5 foretells that after dispersion, the Lord will gather Israel again from all nations. Isaiah 11:11–12 says the Lord "shall set his hand again the second time to recover the remnant of his people." Ezekiel 36:24 declares, "For I will take you from among the heathen, and gather you out of all countries, and will bring you into your own land." Ezekiel 37:21–22 reiterates that promise and links it to national reunification. The valley of dry bones in Ezekiel 37:1–14 further symbolizes Israel's national revival, first physically and then spiritually. These texts show both a national regathering and a future spiritual renewal centered in God's covenant faithfulness.

The New Testament also points to a future remnant of Jewish believers who will turn to Christ during the tribulation. Revelation 7 distinguishes between two groups: first, the 144,000 sealed from "all the tribes of the children of Israel" (Revelation 7:4–8), and second, "a great multitude, which no man could number, of all nations, and kindreds, and people, and tongues" standing before the throne (Revelation 7:9). When asked who these are, the answer is given: "These are they which came out of great tribulation" (Revelation 7:14). The text clearly distinguishes the 144,000 Israelites from the innumerable multitude from the nations, yet both are connected to God's saving work during that period. This beautifully corresponds to Zechariah 8:23, where the nations are shown attaching themselves to the people through whom God is visibly working.

According to this understanding, during the tribulation, many Jews will finally recognize Jesus as the true Messiah. Their present partial blindness, described in Romans 11:25, will not last forever. When they believe the gospel of Christ, they will be saved without the commandments that are given to the church to be baptized and filled with the Holy Spirit, but believe and confess what the Jews refused to do in the life and time of Jesus on earth. They will be saved by their faith in the Lord Jesus Christ. Romans 10:9 says, "That if thou shalt confess with thy mouth the Lord Jesus, and shalt believe in thine heart that God hath raised him from the dead, thou shalt be saved." Verse 13 adds, "For whosoever shall call upon the name of the Lord shall be saved." The basis for salvation is never ethnic identity, law-keeping, or tribal descent, but faith in the crucified and risen Messiah. Thus, even in the tribulation, Jews who refuse the mark of the beast and turn to Jesus are not saved by Jewishness, but by grace through faith in Christ.

Other prophetic texts reinforce Israel's central role in the end times. Luke 21:24 says Jerusalem will be "trodden down of the Gentiles, until the times of the Gentiles be fulfilled." Zechariah 12:2–3 predicts that Jerusalem will become "a cup of trembling" and "a burdensome stone for all people," showing that the city itself will remain the focal point of international conflict. Zechariah 14:2–4 speaks of the nations gathering against Jerusalem and of the Lord Himself returning to stand upon the Mount of Olives. Acts 1:11–12 connects Jesus' ascension from the Mount of Olives with His promised return. Thus, the same region that witnessed His rejection and ascension will witness His glorious return and deliverance of Israel.

The climax of this prophetic program is the visible return of Jesus Christ. Matthew 24:29–31 says that after the tribulation, the Son of man will appear in heaven and gather His elect. Revelation 19:11–16 portrays Christ returning as King of kings and Lord of lords. Zechariah 14 shows Him delivering Jerusalem and reigning over all the earth. At that time, the remnant of Israel will say in faith what Jesus anticipated in Matthew 23:39: "Blessed is he that cometh in the name of the Lord." What was once rejected will then be received. The Messiah, whom many did not recognize at His first coming, will be embraced at His second.

Therefore, the biblical record does not support replacement ideas that erase Israel from God's prophetic plan, nor does it support doctrines that claim divine covenant identity while rejecting the clear testimony of Scripture concerning the Jewish people. The prophets, the Gospels, Paul's epistles, and Revelation all testify that ethnic Israel and Jerusalem retain a central place in God's end-time program. The Jewish people will experience unparalleled trouble, yet a remnant will repent, believe in the Lord Jesus Christ, and be saved. The nations will witness that God is with them, and the Messiah will reign from Jerusalem exactly as the Scriptures have foretold.

## Conclusion

This manuscript has argued that the central claims of the self-proclaimed Black Hebrew Israelite movement fail both historically and biblically. Its burden has not been to deny the suffering of African Americans, to minimize the crimes of slavery and segregation, or to erase Africa from the biblical world. Rather, its burden has been to show that real pain does not make a false genealogy true, and that righteous indignation does not transform speculative ideology into sound exegesis. A doctrine may arise from wounded memory and still be mistaken in its reading of history, its handling of Scripture, and its understanding of the gospel.

The gospel does not ask you to locate your worth in a hidden genealogy. It tells you the truth about your dignity (made in God's image), your need (all have sinned), and God's rescue (Christ died for our sins and rose again). Any movement that makes ethnic status the key to salvation offers a counterfeit hope. Biblical faith can honor African history without rewriting it as Israel, and it can honor Israel's story without denying the Jewish people. In Christ, God is making one new humanity redeemed by grace, called to holiness, and sent to proclaim reconciliation.

God did not intend for the nation of Israel to be of one race. It only started as a tribe and would flourish into the prophecy that all nations would call upon his name. It does not matter if you are an Israelite biologically or spiritually by becoming a proselyte or convert. As long as you name the name of the LORD, you shall be saved or rescued from the penalty of your sins. God told Abraham, "Nether shall thy name any more be called Abram, but thy name shall be Abraham; for a father of many nations have I made thee" (KJV, Gen. 17:5). Teaching concepts outside the Bible creates a Tower of Babel of information and an insurmountable amount of confusion among believers.

Historically, the manuscript has shown that the recognizable Black Hebrew Israelite movement is a modern phenomenon, shaped in the crucible of post-emancipation trauma, Black religious innovation, racial humiliation, and the search for dignity in a hostile society. That background helps explain the movement's emotional force, but it does not prove an ancient pedigree. Chapter 1, therefore, situates BHI origins where the evidence places them: within the modern history of the Americas rather than within an unbroken chain from ancient Israel to West Africa to the trans-Atlantic slave trade.

The biblical case collapses for similar reasons. Chapter 2 demonstrated that "Israel" in Scripture is a covenant people constituted by divine promise, covenant obligation, and redemptive purpose, not a modern racial category mapped onto skin color. The Old Testament itself includes outsiders by faith and covenant loyalty, and the New Testament intensifies that truth by gathering Jew and Gentile into one people in Christ. Chapter 3 then showed that Deuteronomy 28 cannot responsibly be turned into a coded newspaper of modern Atlantic slavery. The covenant curses belong to the historical world of ancient Israel's obedience, rebellion, exile, and judgment; they cannot be made to say whatever racial ideology requires.

Chapters 4 and 5 exposed the weakness of the movement's most popular historical "proofs." The myth of the so-called lost tribes has been repeatedly expanded far beyond what the evidence can bear, and modern attempts to identify present-day populations as those tribes usually depend on desire, legend, and retroactive imagination rather than verifiable history. In the same way, appeals to genealogy charts, selective cultural parallels, haplogroups, and amateur etymologies do not establish descent from Jacob. These methods often begin with the conclusion and then gather fragments that appear to support it. That is not careful scholarship; it is confirmation bias dressed in prophetic language.

The deepest error, however, is theological. Chapters 6 and 7 argued that many BHI presentations do not merely get history wrong; they preach another message of salvation. When ethnic pedigree, Torah observance, or tribal identification becomes a condition of justification, the sufficiency of Christ is displaced. The apostles preach repentance and faith in the crucified and risen Lord, not redemption by bloodline. Scripture does not authorize a racial monopoly on election, nor does it permit the inversion of white supremacy into black supremacy. In Christ, the dividing wall is broken down, and the one new humanity is formed by grace, not ancestry.

This is why the manuscript has also insisted that Africa must be treated with historical integrity rather than ideological exploitation. Chapter 8 showed that Africa is already present in Scripture in concrete and dignified ways and that African civilizations possessed depth, antiquity, and achievement without any need for borrowed Israelite origins. West African peoples occupied West Africa long before Israel emerged as a nation, and the populations swept into the Atlantic slave trade came from many distinct ethnic, linguistic, and political communities. To collapse that complexity into a single hidden-Israel narrative is not to honor Africa, but to flatten it.

Chapter 9 brought these themes together by exposing the mechanics of misinformation: word games masquerading as exegesis, isolated quotations presented without context, redefinitions of basic biblical terms, and conspiratorial claims used to shield weak arguments from correction. This kind of error spreads because it offers certainty, grievance, and identity all at once. Yet rhetoric is not evidence, and repeated assertion is not proof. The test of truth remains the same: historical claims must be examined by sound historical method, and biblical claims must be judged by context, grammar, canon, and the gospel of Jesus Christ.

For that reason, the pastoral burden of this manuscript is as important as its historical and exegetical burden. The answer to centuries of degradation is not a new doctrine of ethnic chosenness, and the answer to lies told about black people is not the construction of a counter-myth that enslaves its hearers to resentment, superiority, and false hope. The wounds that made this movement attractive are real. They should be answered with truth, justice, dignity, and the lordship of Christ, not with teachings that harden pride, divide neighbors, and obscure the grace of God.

The final word, then, is not hidden ancestry but revealed gospel. This manuscript rejects the central claims of Black Hebrew Israelite doctrine because they are historically unsubstantiated, biblically distorted, and spiritually dangerous. But it does so to point to something better: the true Messiah, the true fulfillment of the covenant, and the true people of God, gathered from every tribe, tongue, people, and nation through faith in Jesus Christ. That vision is larger than racial myth, more honest than ideological propaganda, and more healing than any counterfeit promise of bloodline redemption.

# Index of Bible Scriptures by Manuscript Section

*Grouped by manuscript section. Unless marked NET, scripture citations follow the manuscript's stated default use of the KJV. Chapter-only references and manuscript-form citations have been retained as cited.*

**NET:** Titus 3:9; 1 Timothy 1:3–4.

## Chapter 6: The Gospel versus Law-Based Ethnic Salvation

**KJV:** Galatians 2:16; Galatians 3:10; Galatians 3:21–22; Romans 8:1–4; Matthew 5:17; Acts 15; Isaiah 53; Isaiah 61; Psalm 40:7; Hebrews 10:7; Ephesians 2:15; Ephesians 2:15–17; Hebrews 12:24; Colossians 2:14; John 4:24; John 14:6; Romans 1:3; Revelation 21:3; 1 John 4:3; Philippians 2:7; Romans 8:3; John 1:14; Romans 8:14; 2 Corinthians 3:17; Joel 2:28; Hosea 11:1; Matthew 2:15; Jeremiah 14:2; Jeremiah 8:21; Lamentations 5:10; Zechariah 6:6; Song of Solomon 1:5–6.

## Chapter 7: Race, Salvation, and the One New Humanity

**KJV:** Acts 17:30–31; Genesis 12:3; Isaiah 2:2–4; Ephesians 3:6; 2 Chronicles 11:3; Ezra 2:70; Ezra 3:11; Ezra 8:35; Ezra 10:25; Nehemiah 12:47; Malachi 1:1; Genesis 12:1–2; Mark 7:26; Romans 3:29; John 1:11; Matthew 13:58; Mark 6:5; John 3:16; Luke 14:27; Matthew 28:19; Mark 16:15; Revelation 7:9; Zechariah 8:23; Romans 7:14; Romans 11; Romans 11:11–15; Romans 11:17; Romans 11:25; Galatians 3:28–29; Romans 1:16; Ephesians 3:8; Acts 10:34; Romans 9:25; Romans 10:1; Isaiah 46:9; Joel 2:28; Acts 2:8–11, 16; Colossians 2:11.

**NET:** Romans 2:28–29; Romans 9:6–8.

## Chapter 8: Africa, the Bible, and Historical Integrity

**KJV:** Acts 8:26–40; Jeremiah 36:14.

## Chapter 9: Misinformation: Definitions, Etymologies, and Propaganda

**KJV:** Acts 4:36; Acts 13:1; Exodus 19:6; Mark 7:26.

## Chapter 10: Israel in Prophecy

**KJV:** Revelation 11:3–8, Daniel 9:27, 2 Thessalonians 2:3–4 Matthew 24:15, John 5:43, Exodus 20:3–4, Daniel 12:1, Jeremiah 30:7, Zechariah 13:8–9, Zechariah 12:10, Romans 11:25–27, Zechariah 8:23 Isaiah 2:2–4, Micah 4:1–3, Zechariah 14:16, Deuteronomy 30:1–5, Isaiah 11:11–12, Ezekiel 36:24,  Ezekiel 37:21–22, Ezekiel 37:1–14, Revelation 7:4–8, Revelation 7:9-14, Romans 10:9,13, Zechariah 12:2–3, Zechariah

14:2–4, Acts 1:11–12, Matthew 24:29–31,  Revelation 19:11–16, Matthew 23:39:

**Conclusion**

    **KJV:** Deuteronomy 28, Genesis 17:5.

# Bibliography

Aafreedi, Navras J. "The Tradition of Israelite Descent Among the Pashtuns in India and Its Contemporary Ramifications." In Africana Jewish Journeys: Studies in African Judaism, 202. 2018.

Aafreedi, Navras Jaat. "Claimants of Israelite Descent in South Asia." The Journal of Indo-Judaic Studies 14 (2014).

"Africa in the Bible: Mizraim & Kush." HTML article.

Akrong, A. O. "Trade, Routes, Trade, and Commerce in Pre-Colonial Africa." In Springer Gender, 65–82. Springer, 2019.

Ammann, Birgit. "The Kurdish Jewish Communities: Lost Forever." In Religious Minorities in Kurdistan: Beyond the Mainstream, 271–300. 2014.

Anderson, Chad L. The Storied Landscape of Iroquoia: History, Conquest, and Memory in the Native Northeast. Lincoln: University of Nebraska Press, 2021.

Anti-Defamation League, Center on Extremism. "Hebrews to Negroes: What You Need to Know." November 11, 2022.

Anti-Defamation League. "Extremist Sects Within the Black Hebrew Israelite Movement." New York: Anti-Defamation League, n.d.

"Archaeological Perspective of the Lost Tribes of Israel." The Biblical Archaeologist 6, no. 3 (September 1943): 57–64.

Arsenovic, Daniela. "Population of the World." 2024.

Aster, Shawn Zev. "Transmission of Neo-Assyrian Claims of Empire to Judah in the Late Eighth Century BCE." Hebrew Union College Annual 78 (2007): 1–23.

Austen, Ralph A. Trans-Saharan Africa in World History. Oxford: Oxford University Press, 2010.

Bar-Yosef, Eitan. The Holy Land in English Culture, 1799–1917: Palestine and the Question of Orientalism. Oxford: Oxford University Press, 2005.

Bible History. "The Table of Nations." Web article.

"Black Hebrew Israelites." Wikipedia.

"Black Hebrew Israelites: A Christian Evaluation and Response." CARM.

Bosworth, Albert Brian. Conquest and Empire: The Reign of Alexander the Great. Cambridge: Cambridge University Press, 1993.

Buijs, Gina. "Black Jews in the Northern Province: A Study of Ethnic Identity in South Africa." Ethnic and Racial Studies 21, no. 4 (1998): 661–682.

Butts, Jimmy. "The Origin and Insufficiency of the Black Hebrew Israelite Movement." Christian Research Journal 39, no. 4 (2016).

Cogley, Richard W. "Some Other Kinde of Being and Condition: The Controversy in Mid-Seventeenth-Century England over the Peopling of Ancient America." Journal of the History of Ideas 68, no. 1 (2007): 35–56.

Conrad, David C. *Empires of Medieval West Africa: Ghana, Mali, and Songhay*. New York: Infobase Publishing, 2010.

Cottrell-Boyce, Aidan. *Israelism in Modern Britain*. London: Routledge, 2020.

Crome, Andrew. "Politics and Eschatology: Reassessing the Appeal of the 'Jewish Indian' Theory in England and New England in the 1650s." Journal of Religious History 40, no. 3 (2015): 326–346.

Davidson, Basil. *The African Past: Chronicles from Antiquity to Modern Times*. London: Longman, 1964.

Dorman, Jacob S. *Chosen People: The Rise of American Black Israelite Religions*. Oxford: Oxford University Press, 2012.

Duling, Dennis C. "Ethnicity, Ethnocentrism, and the Matthean Ethnos." Biblical Theology Bulletin 35, no. 4 (2005): 125–143.

Dundon, Alison. "Babala and the Bible: Israel and a 'Messianic Church' in Papua New Guinea." Oceania 85, no. 3 (2015): 327–341.

Egorova, Yulia. "The Proof Is in the Genes? Jewish Responses to DNA Research." Culture and Religion 10, no. 2 (2009): 159–175.

Ejiofor, Promise Frank. "Jewishness without Jews? Ontological Security, Ethnonationalism, and the Social Power of Analogical Reasoning in Postcolonial Nigeria." Nationalities Papers (2022): 1–29.

Elazar, Gideon, and Miriam Billig. "The Immigration and Strategic Assimilation of Bene Menashe: A Zomian Jewish Community in Israel." Asian Studies Review 49, no. 2 (2025): 424–442.

Ellinghaus, Katherine. "Absorbing the 'Aboriginal Problem': Controlling Interracial Marriage in Australia in the Late Nineteenth and Early Twentieth Centuries." Aboriginal History 27 (2003): 183–207.

Eltis, David. "A Brief Overview of the Trans-Atlantic Slave Trade." Voyages: The Trans-Atlantic Slave Trade Database (2007).

Encyclopedia Britannica. "Gentile." Last modified July 20, 1998.

Fischel, Walter J. "Cochin in Jewish History: Prolegomena to a History of the Jews in India." Proceedings of the American Academy for Jewish Research 30 (1962).

Fontein, Joost, and Neil L. Norman. "The Silence of Great Zimbabwe: Contested Landscapes and the Power of Heritage." 2009.

Gaca, Kathy L., and Laurence L. Welborn, eds. *Early Patristic Readings of Romans*. London: A&C Black, 2005.

Gamkrelidze, Thomas V., and Vjačeslav V. Ivanov. "The Migrations of Tribes Speaking the Indo-European Dialects from Their Original Homeland in the Near East to Their Historical Habitations in Eurasia." Soviet Studies in History 22, nos. 1–2 (1983): 53–95.

Gelston, Anthony. "Universalism in Second Isaiah." The Journal of Theological Studies 43, no. 2 (1992): 377–398.

Goldschmidt, E., and T. Cohen. "Inter-Ethnic Mixture among the Communities of Israel." In Cold Spring Harbor Symposia on Quantitative Biology, vol. 29. Cold Spring Harbor, NY: Cold Spring Harbor Laboratory Press, 1964.

Gow, Andrew. The Red Jews: Antisemitism in an Apocalyptic Age, 1200–1600. Leiden: Brill, 1995.

Handman, Courtney. "Israelite Genealogies and Christian Commitment: The Limits of Language Ideologies in Guhu-Samane Christianity." Anthropological Quarterly 84, no. 3 (2011): 655–677.

Herzstein, Robert E. The Nazis. Alexandria, VA: Time-Life Books, 1980.

Hodes, Joseph R. "The Bene Israel and the 'Who Is a Jew' Controversy in Israel." In Who Is a Jew? Reflections on History, Religion, and Culture, 169–192. 2014.

Huddleston, Lee Eldridge. Origins of the American Indians: European Concepts, 1492–1729. Austin: University of Texas Press, 2015.

Imhoff, Sarah, and Hillary Kaell. "Lineage Matters: DNA, Race, and Gene Talk in Judaism and Messianic Judaism." Religion and American Culture 27, no. 1 (2017): 95–127.

Isaac, Walter. "Locating Afro-American Judaism: A Critique of White Normativity." In A Companion to African-American Studies. Wiley, 2006.

Kahn, Dan'el. "The History of Kush—An Outline." In The Power of Walls: Fortifications in Ancient Northeastern Africa, Colloquium Africanum 5. 2013.

Kaplan, Steven. The Beta Israel (Falasha) in Ethiopia: From Earliest Times to the Twentieth Century. New York: New York University Press, 1992.

Kaplan, Steven. "Genealogies and Gene-Ideologies: The Legitimacy of the Beta Israel (Falasha)." Social Identities 12, no. 4 (2006): 447–455.

Khan, Hameed Ullah, and Nasir Ahmed. "A Genealogical Study of the Origin of Pashtuns." In the International Conference on Intelligent Computing. Berlin and Heidelberg: Springer, 2013.

Kosba, May T. The Race Question: Egyptian Intellectualism on the Periphery of the African Diaspora. Dissertation, 2022.

Kurewa, John Wesley Zwomunondiita. African Religion: The Quarry of the Rock of Monotheism. Upper Room Books, 2016.

Levin, Ayala. Architecture and Development: Israeli Construction in Sub-Saharan Africa and the Settler Colonial Imagination, 1958–1973. 2022.

Marciak, Michał. Izates and Helena of Adiabene: A Study on Literary Traditions and History. 2012.

May, Herbert G. "Archaeological News and Views: The Ten Lost Tribes." The Biblical Archaeologist 6, no. 4 (1943): 55–60.

McLeod, Nicholas C. Practicing Pan-Africanism: West Indians and Governance in Kwame Nkrumah's Ghana. 2020.

McLeod, Norman. Epitome of the Ancient History of Japan. Yokohama: Author, 1878.

Merdinger, Jane, Jesse A. Hoover, and Nancy Weatherwax. Religion at Carthage, 800 BCE–439 CE: From Baal-Hammon to Christ. Leiden: Brill, 2025.

Miller, Michael T. Black Hebrew Israelites. Cambridge: Cambridge University Press, 2024.

Miller, Michael T. "Black Judaism(s) and the Hebrew Israelites." Religion Compass 13, no. 11 (2019): e12346.

Mohamed, Hani Abdirachid. "African Civilization: From Ancient Kingdoms to Modern Societies." International Journal of Social Science and Human Research 6, no. 6 (2023): 3294–3303.

Monges, Miriam Ma'at-Ka-Re. Kush: An Afrocentric Perspective. PhD diss., Temple University, 1995.

Monteiro, John M. Blacks of the Land: Indian Slavery, Settler Society, and the Portuguese Colonial Enterprise in South America. Cambridge: Cambridge University Press, 2018.

Morrow, William S. "Ancient Near Eastern Treaties/Loyalty Oaths and Biblical Law." In The Oxford Handbook of Biblical Law. Oxford: Oxford University Press, 2019.

New English Translation Bible.

Newland, Lynda. "The Lost Tribes of Israel—and the Genesis of Christianity in Fiji: Missionary Notions of Fijian Origin from 1835 to Cession and Beyond." Oceania 85, no. 3 (2015): 256–270.

Obikili, Nonso. "The Trans-Atlantic Slave Trade and Local Political Fragmentation in Africa." The Economic History Review 69, no. 4 (2016): 1157–1177.

Ostrer, Harry. "A Genetic View of Jewish History." Nature Genetics 40, no. 4 (2008): S1–S2.

Painter, Nell Irvin. The History of White People. New York: W. W. Norton, 2011.

Perry, Rufus L. The Cushite; or, The Descendants of Ham, as Found in the Sacred Scriptures and in the Writings of Ancient Historians and Poets, from Noah to the Christian Era. Springfield, MA: Willey & Co., 1893.

Pickrell, Joseph K., and David Reich. "Toward a New History and Geography of Human Genes Informed by Ancient DNA." Trends in Genetics 30, no. 9 (2014): 377–389.

Rabin, Anthony. The Adiabene Narrative in the Jewish Antiquities of Josephus. DPhil diss., University of Oxford, 2017.

Rimmer, Harry. The Magnificence of Jesus: A Study in Christology. Grand Rapids, MI: Wm. B. Eerdmans, 1953.

Salm, Steven J., and Toyin Falola. Culture and Customs of Ghana. Westport, CT: Greenwood Press, 2002.

Salmond, Anne. "Maori Epistemologies." In Reason and Morality, 237–260. Routledge, 2003.

Samra, Myer. "The Benei Menashe: Choosing Judaism in North East India." The Journal of Indo-Judaic Studies 12 (2012): 45–57.

Sandoval-Velasco, Marcela, et al. "The Genetic Origins of Saint Helena's Liberated Africans." bioRxiv (2019): 787515.

Setiawati, D., N. K. Ramadani, and S. Lestari. "The Contribution of Ancient Egypt Civilization to Life in the World." Journal of Religion and Social Change 1, no. 1 (2024): 1–10.

Shapira, Anita. "The Bible and Israeli Identity." AJS Review 28, no. 1 (2004): 11–41.

Smooha, Sammy. "Jewish Ethnicity in Israel: Symbolic or Real?" In Jews in Israel: Contemporary Social and Cultural Patterns 1 (2004): 47–80.

Stanizai, Zaman. "Are Pashtuns the Lost Tribe of Israel?" 2023.

Strong, James. Strong's Exhaustive Concordance of the Bible.

The Holy Bible, King James Version.

"The Myth of the Lost Tribes." Unpublished document.

"The Unbiblical Teachings of the Black Hebrew Israelite Movement (Part Two)." PDF article.

Tobolowsky, Andrew. The Myth of the Twelve Tribes of Israel. Cambridge: Cambridge University Press, 2022.

University of California, Davis. "What Are the Myths and Facts About Hebrew Israelites?"

Uzukwu, E. Elochukwu. "Igbo World and Ultimate Reality and Meaning." Ultimate Reality and Meaning 5, no. 3 (1982): 188–209.

Wellhausen, Julius. Prolegomena to the History of Ancient Israel. Edinburgh: A. and C. Black, 1885.

West, Emily, and Erin Shearer. "Fertility Control, Shared Nurturing, and Dual Exploitation: The Lives of Enslaved Mothers in the Antebellum United States." In Motherhood, Childlessness, and the Care of Children in Atlantic Slave Societies, 117–131. Routledge, 2020.

Whatley, Warren, and Rob Gillezeau. "The Slave Trade and Ethnic Stratification in Africa." Paper presented at Understanding African Poverty over the Longue Durée Conference, Accra, 2010.

Whitelam, Keith W. "The History of Israel: Foundations of Israel." In Text in Context, 376–402. 2000.

Woldekiros, Helina Solomon. The Boundaries of Ancient Trade: Kings, Commoners, and the Aksumite Salt Trade of Ethiopia. Louisville: University Press of Colorado, 2023.

Younger, K. Lawson. "The Deportations of the Israelites." *Journal of Biblical Literature* 117, no. 2 (1998): 201–227.

## About the Author:

Dr. James L. Perry Sr. was born and raised in Saginaw, MI, to James and Earnestine Perry. He excelled in athletics growing up, which allowed him to play collegiate sports at Central State University and Tuskegee University. After attending a church revival at the Apostolic Faith Mission while attending Tuskegee University in Tuskegee, AL, he was converted by the power of GOD. This is where he began preaching and teaching the Gospel of Jesus Christ, serving faithfully at the Apostolic Faith Mission as an Associate Minister and in many other ministerial roles. In 2001, he began aiding Bishop George F. Austin in the Louisiana District Council of the PAW, Inc., and was ordained an Elder of the Pentecostal Assemblies of the World, Inc. in August of 2003. Since then, Bro. Perry has evangelized in over twenty of the 50 States and forty cities, including Canada. In November 2008, he founded The Church by Christ Jesus in Columbus, Ohio, and pastored for seven years. He is married to the lovely Cynthia Perry and has three beautiful children. Bro. Perry has enjoyed years of mentorship under the tutelage of Dr. Johnny James (The Walking Bible), who has greatly influenced his ministry and accompanied him in evangelism. Brother Perry's studies include a B.A. in Psychology from Tuskegee University, a B.A. in Pastoral Ministry from Aenon Bible College, a Post-Baccalaureate degree in Mental Health Counseling, a Master of Science in Psychology from Grand Canyon University, and a Master's and Ph.D. in Integrative Public Policy and Development at Tuskegee University. He is currently completing a Master of Divinity at Regent University.

For readings and book signings, contact the author at jperryministries@seeksearchstudy.com.

SEEK SEARCH STUDY
TRUTH SEEKING MINISTRIES

www.ingramcontent.com/pod-product-compliance
Lightning Source LLC
Chambersburg PA
CBHW071447130726
47997CB00006B/2266